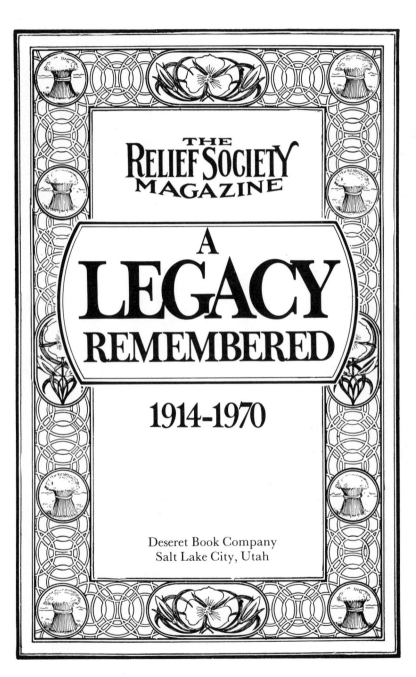

THE
RELIEF SOCIETY
MAGAZINE

A
LEGACY
REMEMBERED

1914-1970

Deseret Book Company
Salt Lake City, Utah

Contents

Preface

In this one hundred and fortieth anniversary year of Relief Society, we pay tribute to Latter-day Saint women, celebrating a "Legacy—Remembered and Renewed." Relief Society, the gift of God to women, was organized by the Prophet Joseph Smith in 1842. In succeeding years, benefiting greatly from priesthood blessing and direction, it has responded to the needs of women and their families in helping to build the kingdom.

As part of this anniversary celebration, we are pleased to publish selections from the *Relief Society Magazine,* which is one of the great legacies of women in the Church. In this volume you will read of the challenges and triumphs of Relief Society sisters through years that spanned the establishment of rural communities in the valleys of the mountains, to a globe-encompassing membership representing many cultures.

Through this publication we remember with pride and gratitude the work of hundreds of thousands of women in the cause of Relief Society. With renewed dedication we go forward now with over one and a half million members to meet the challenges of our day and realize the joy of membership in this glorious society of Saints.

GENERAL RELIEF SOCIETY PRESIDENCY

Barbara B. Smith
Marian R. Boyer
Shirley W. Thomas

Relief Society General Board, 1982. Seated, left to right: Mayola R. Miltenberger, secretary-treasurer; Marian R. Boyer, first counselor; Barbara B. Smith, president; Shirley W. Thomas, second counselor; Amy Y. Valentine. Center row: Mary F. Foulger, Joy F. Evans, Helen L. Goates, Helen B. Gibbons, Janath R. Cannon, Ruth T. Walker, Beverly J. Pond, Miriam B. Milne, Ramona H. Barker, Junko I. Shimizu. Back row: Ann S. Reese, Barbara W. Winder, Arlene J. Flanders, Margaret Smoot, Jewel J. Cutler, Marian R. Johnson, Arlene S. Kirton, Helen W. Jeppson, Carol L. Clark, Addie Fuhriman, Bonna A. Britton, Marjorie Y. Nelson, Elaine L. Jack. Absent when picture was taken: Anne Osborn.

Livingston, Terri Mitchell, Shirlene Pope, Charlotte Prante, Fran Richardson, Joan Robson, Mary Tallmadge, Carolyn Wright, and Leslie Wuthrich.

From Rexburg: Janet L. Allen, Irma Anderson, Colleen Barton, Marjorie O. Bennion, Ruth H. Biddulph, Moana Boyle, Donna S. Bright, Gayle B. Brown, Jean C. Brown, Catherine Burnham, Verla J. Chapman, Joanne F. Christensen, LaRae Clarke, Carol Clements, Judie R. Dresen, Pollie Fitch, Dianna D. Forbis, Anne M. Forsnes, Vicki Gehring, Gay Grant, Harriet Grass, Lonnie Hackworth, Joan T. Haeberle, Iris H. Hathaway, Candyce Howells, Enid B. Hunter, Geraldine M. Jacobs, Dorla R. Jenkins, Cleo Johnson, Inga Johnson, Miken O. Johnson, Lisa Kartchner, Donna Jean L. Kinghorn, Helen Lamprecht, Merlyn M. Larson, Erma H. Magleby, Mary K. Messer, Linda Miller, Jessie P. Morrell, Lenore C. Passey, Ingvi L. Pearson, Merena D. Reed, Cheryl V. Reeser, Beverly W. Ricks, Carolyn Roberts, Carolyn H. Robison, Mary R. Rydalch, Kayleen Scott, Kay B. Stubbs, Ann M. Thomas, Carolyn S. Thompson, Etta G. Thompson, Lera P. Thomson, Lola B. Walters, Alanna Whittier, Sharon O. Williams, Sharol D. Wilson, and Juanita J. Wulf.

From St. George, Utah: Ruth C. Hafen.

Editorial assistant: Blythe D. Thatcher.

Proofreaders: Alice C. Cannon, Lois C. Clark.

In Appreciation

In the fall of 1979, the Relief Society presidency asked Shirley A. Cazier of Logan, Utah, and Marie K. Hafen of Rexburg, Idaho, to review the *Relief Society Magazine* and select material worthy of republication. Because the magazine stretched from 1914 to 1970, and there were 684 monthly issues, we invited eighty-one women to help. Old and young, single and married, new converts and fifty-year Relief Society veterans, the sisters brought the richness of varying amounts of formal education and numerous backgrounds.

The individual issues and bound volumes of the magazine have been constant companions for all of us over these past years. They have traveled to vacation spots and meetings and have cluttered family rooms, bedrooms, and dining room tables.

As we compiled the sisters' observations, certain "gems" began to emerge through repeated readings by concurring readers. From these Sister Cazier, Sister Hafen, and Carol L. Clark, a Relief Society general board member who wrote her doctoral dissertation about Relief Society and was asked by the Relief Society general presidency to head the final editing and publication preparation, chose the pieces found in these pages. For every one of these items, there are three or four others in the files, just as engaging, thought-provoking, and uplifting.

We express our thanks and love for those who read and evaluated so effectively and willingly. They include:

From Logan: Elaine Alder, Barbara Allred, Julia Barrett, Carolyn Bentley, Charlotte Bleh, Helen Cannon, Ruth Champneys, Vera Christensen, Irene Eastmond, Barbara Fjeldsted, Joan Griffin, Bonnie Hart, Anna Keogh, Nancy Law, Kay

Introduction

In December 1970, after a fifty-seven-year history, publication of the *Relief Society Magazine* came to an end. Although many of the 298,250 subscribers looked forward to the inauguration of a new magazine that would bring interests of men and women of the Church together, there were those who could not help but look back. The *Relief Society Magazine* had been an outgrowth of the *Woman's Exponent,* and together they had spanned a period of nearly one hundred years. Such a tradition for women would not die without a degree of sadness. One eighty-four-year-old woman unknowingly expressed the feelings of many Relief Society sisters in 1970 when she bid the magazine farewell for reasons of her own:

> Dear Relief Society Magazine: It is with regret and tears that I must say good-bye. My sight is so bad and no repairs can be given it, so I cannot read you anymore. For thirty years and more I have enjoyed you, but now I am unable to read the wonderful stories and articles. Good-bye Magazine. I hate so to see you go. . . . (Vol. 56, no. 3 [Mar. 1969], p. 162.)

Now over a decade later we have compiled a volume of some of the best selections from this magazine which so many women loved so well. Since 1982 marks the 140th anniversary of the founding of Relief Society, we believe this publication is most appropriate. In a real sense this book is a celebration of future promise and past legacy, for it is perhaps the single best barometer of the temperaments and attitudes, joys and woes of generations of Mormon women.

Originally the *Relief Society Magazine*'s major purpose was to provide a forum for lessons. In 1914 the *Relief Society Guide* and *Relief Society Bulletin* introduced uniform "guide" lessons written at Church headquarters, thus superseding the *Woman's Expo-*

nent, which had served women under the editorship of Lula Greene Richards, 1872-1877, and Emmeline B. Wells, 1877-1914. Sister Wells, general president when the *Relief Society Magazine* started, was the last of the "old guard." Having lived through the Nauvoo period, in a new century she was a literal link with the past.

While President Wells provided much of the continuity and ballast needed for the fledgling *Relief Society Magazine,* Susa Young Gates, Brigham Young's daughter and the first editor of the magazine, brought fresh wind for the sails. In the first issue she wrote:

> It is impossible for us to be sure what any child of ours may become. How much more impossible, then, to forecast what shall be the future, the final character, of this literary infant, newly-born. If the Editor of this enterprise might shape its policy and fashion its fulfilment, she would have this magazine filled with the Spirit of the Lord from cover to cover. In order to do this, no article should be published which would encourage vanity, hurtful luxury, sin, or any evil passion of the human breast. Rather would we make of this magazine a beacon light of hope, beauty, and charity.
>
> The Christian world have all the virtues. They practice many of the moral precepts of true religion; they are charitable, kind, honest, and intelligent. They lack one thing, and one thing only, and that is the Gospel of Jesus Christ in its fulness, taught by those having authority. It is therefore, the spirit and genius of the Gospel which we would like to develop and expound brightly, attractively, cheerfully, and hopefully, to the readers of *The Relief Society Magazine.* (Vol. 2, no. 1 [Jan. 1915], p. 38.)

In 1922 Editor Gates explained that the editorial policy for a considerable period had been "to print articles, poems, stories, and departments written by Latter-day Saint women (rarely men) for Latter-day Saint readers." She explained:

> Life's problems, as they affect the mature women, touch the members of this Society closely. . . . The treatment of these problems or plots or ideas in verse, story or article may be scholarly and polished, or amateur and crude. But when two articles or poems are side by side there are two standards by which we judge and choose: one is, the spirit that pervades it; second, the manner of its expression. As between a cold, spiritless, finished story, and a halting, crudely-told tale, breathing a testimony of the gospel from start to finish, we choose the inspired story, if it is at all possible; we may have to dress it up . . . with our red and blue pencil. . . . Above all, We present to this greatest of all women's organizations the spirit and letter of the instructions and conferences taught and

held by the Presidency and General Board of the Society itself; and news of Relief Society women, and of the Relief Society everywhere; these together with the lessons in our Guide make up Your *Relief Society Magazine*. (Vol. 9, no. 1 [Jan. 1922], p. 49.)

By 1922 the ground rules were firmly established, the precedent cemented fast. It was clear that the Relief Society leaders hoped their publication would bless the lives of their sisters. In subsequent years several "departments" (regular columns) came and went, format and name changes occurred, but the magazine adhered to its original intentions and editorial policy.

From our own editorial perspective, we concur that the best testament to the prowess and diligence of the women who worked on the magazine is the love so many have expressed for it. Representing, as we do, single and married, career women and mothers in the home, and having given considerable time to this project, we have found we also have been moved, inspired, and uplifted by much of what we have read.

Based on our research, we have selected articles representative of the gamut of womanhood and Relief Society work, yet salient for today's Latter-day Saint woman. We hope to maintain the integrity of the documents by keeping the original punctuation, capitalization, spelling, and colloquial language with only minor corrections of typographical errors or to enhance clarity.

The book cover and title page harken back to the first decades of the *Relief Society Magazine*'s publication. While we have updated information on the title page, we have kept the original quotation from President Joseph F. Smith. This statement was part of a letter he wrote to the Relief Society to congratulate and encourage the leadership as they launched the magazine. The Relief Society general presidency used it in their first editorial, entitled "Greetings and Sentiments," in January 1915 and kept it as part of the title page for many years.

The cover motifs were—and are—symbolic. Sego lilies, a reminder of dire days and women's resourcefulness, were utilized extensively on magazine covers and in other graphics. The wheat became part of Relief Society in 1876 when Brigham Young asked women to gather it against a day of need; sheaves of wheat on the Relief Society Building facade still represent a reaping and a planting. The section page design itself was one of the earliest and best covers ever designed for the *Magazine*.

We leave this project with a keener sense of the timely nature of Relief Society work and the timeless qualities of the organization itself. There is a profoundness about seekers of truth: there have been many in Relief Society, and we are better women for having learned of them.

Carol L. Clark, Editor
Shirley A. Cazier, Associate Editor
Marie K. Hafen, Associate Editor

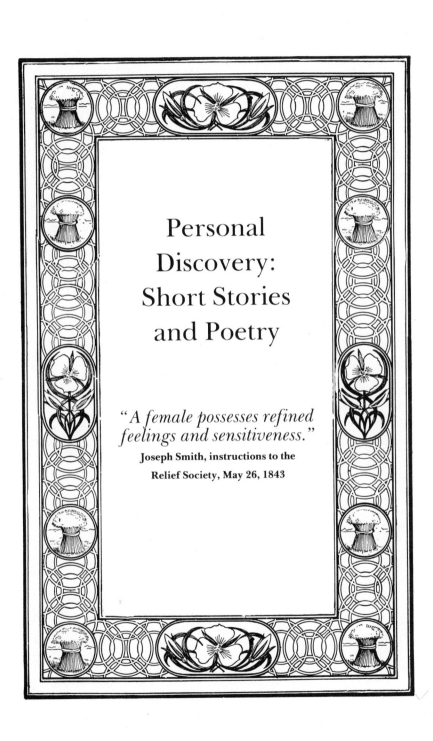

Personal Discovery: Short Stories and Poetry

"A female possesses refined feelings and sensitiveness."

Joseph Smith, instructions to the
Relief Society, May 26, 1843

Personal Discovery

Through the years the *Relief Society Magazine* published countless stories and poems, providing an outlet for the writings of numerous women. Creative women also received special encouragement through the magazine's contests. In fact, the Relief Society poem contest, which began in 1923 as the Eliza R. Snow Memorial Poem Contest, is the oldest writing competition in the Church. During its centennial year in 1942, Relief Society introduced a short story contest. A song contest announced in 1933 was quickly discontinued when the 163 entries failed to measure up to the judges' expectations. It was reopened in 1968, and winners were announced in the *Relief Society Magazine* for two years.

When the magazine ended, the Relief Society poem and song competitions were continued in the *Ensign*. The short stories were made part of an all-Church writing contest.

Although many women won Relief Society contests, three excelled more than any others: in poetry, Eva Willes Wangsgaard; in short story, Alice Morrey Bailey; in song, Ruth Lehenbauer.

Given the wealth of material from these and other contributors, the task of selecting only two stories and a few poems has

been difficult. The stories by Vesta Pierce Crawford and Vangie Mae Blair portray two significant aspects of Relief Society. "Miracle on a March Day" captures one of the greatest Relief Society achievements, that of bringing together a variety of women in a common bond of love and sisterhood. With charm and humor, "To Visit the Sick" reveals Relief Society's cardinal concept of compassionate service.

Vol. 22, no. 10 (Oct. 1935), p. 680.

Miracle on a March Day

By Vesta Pierce Crawford

"An ugly black stove instead of shining white enamel," said Shannon Heath, as she set the frying pan over the blazing wood fire in the kitchen range, "and pancakes instead of waffles."

The pancakes bubbled up and Shannon turned them skillfully. She could do without household conveniences if she had to, but there were certain things that she could not do without. She knew exactly what these things were, but no one else could possibly understand—no one in Utah anyway.

Not even Dan. And he really wanted to understand. She heard him out on the porch splashing water over his face. She could tell when the water spattered on and how it trickled off, and she knew just when he would seize the towel and when the water from the blue granite washbasin would land on the ground. Some men have such an irritating way of washing their faces and soaking their hair. Sometimes Shannon felt that she could not endure the snorting. Maybe, though, it wasn't his way of washing that was so bad. Just the general lack of culture, absence of the finer things.

Dan slammed the door shut. "Is that some March wind, not cold, but fierce, a snow-eating wind. I'll be plowing come tomorrow."

Come tomorrow. He had even forgotten the kind of language he had used when he was a law student back east. The kind of language he had used to impress Shannon when he first knew her back there at the university. Lawyer turned farmer. What a change! Well, she hated farms—especially Utah farms. And Utah people. She was glad that she didn't know many of them.

5

The fewer the better. Two years on the Fremont, and she was acquainted with only a few of the neighbors. But if they were a fair sample of the rest, it was just as well to have very little to do with them.

"Bring on the hotcakes. Do they look good, and Shannon, you're a beaut. That hair. Them eyes."

He thought he saw anger flare suddenly in her dark blue eyes. He looked at the magnificent coil of red hair on the small regal head. A smile now and then and she would be priceless.

"What you going to do today, honey? It's a swell day—snow almost melted, ice broke loose in the creek and crashing down. Hans Gunderson digging a ditch. What you going to do?"

"Clean the lamp chimneys. Wash the separator. Sweep up some mud. Tend the chickens. And if I get time, I'm going to read."

Shannon read too much, but he didn't want to tell her that. And such peculiar reading. Not the plain kind of words he liked. Her books were different. A few days ago he had opened one of her volumes of poems and read a little. The phrases puzzled him. They didn't seem to mean anything. Strange how Shannon enjoyed such books, sitting hours alone reading them over and over again.

"Shan, dear, why don't you come out of the kinks and see a little more of the neighbors? Get acquainted with our native Utah stock. We farmers along the Fremont may not be polished much on the outside, but we're solid clear through."

"Well, sometimes I'd prefer a little polish."

"Shan, don't try to be someone you're not. You were never cut out to be a cynic, a darling like you. I'd like my wife to understand my friends and find out what they're really like."

"The more I see of them, the less I like them."

Shannon pushed back her chair and looked out at Mill Valley—a stretch of hills navy blue with cedars and patched here and there with snow; a canal skirting the hills; then the patterned fields sloping down to the creek. It was rugged and yet peaceful —strange combination. Far away toward the blue mountains she could see the canyon gash—the place where the pioneers had come through when they first saw the Fremont. So Dan had said, and the pioneers thought this the fairest valley under heaven.

Well, they were pioneers with the ability to see paradise in any valley that meant an end to wandering.

"Shan, why don't you pick up and go in town to Relief Society meeting today. Mother was saying last night that the lesson's going to be about literature, Utah poetry."

"Is there any?"

Dan ignored the implication. "Well, they're going to talk about Utah poetry today in the literature lesson. Mother said Flossie Nielson's getting the work ready."

Flossie Nielson! The image of that woman loomed up before Shannon. Flossie Nielson, of all people.

Dan was still pleading. "I'd think just out of curiosity you ought to go."

Maybe she would go. It ought to be humorous to hear Flossie Nielson talk about poetry—Utah poetry, if there was any. And what could these farm women understand about such things? She would go and see.

The March wind billowed the flounce of her blue wool suit. Shannon wore low-heeled brown shoes that left neat little prints along the edge of the road. She walked close to the bank of the creek to watch the loosened ice boulders roll and tumble in the stream. There was a smell of spring in the air, and along Cedar Ridge farmers plowed on the dry hillsides. Shannon felt the wind on her face and the song of the creek in her ears. Springtime in the hill country!

Suddenly Shannon heard a raucous honk. She looked up just in time to see Flossie Nielson back a rattling old car out of the stockyard. Flossie twisted the wheel and brought the car around into the road. With one hand she pushed two little boys down into the back seat. Then she settled the baby girl down into her lap. Her hat was only half on, and the tie on her yellow print dress was still waiting to be done up.

"Want a lift?" she called to Shannon.

The girl in the road turned. Flossie Nielson! But she might as well act grateful.

She climbed into the front seat, and the car lurched forward and leaped along over the ruts.

"I've been more than busy today," explained Flossie. "Had to put the finishing touches on the lesson. And right the last minute

Top: General board under Clarissa Williams, circa 1921.
Bottom: Presidency and board of Louise Y. Robison, 1933.

Tommy pinched his finger in the door and that man of mine brought two cattle buyers home for dinner."

"I don't see how you get time to work in the Relief Society." Shannon was trying to make conversation.

"Time! I don't have time, but I take it. We farm women need Relief Society. It's about our only chance for lovely things. Why, I wouldn't have read a poem these last fifteen years if it had not been for our literary lessons."

Poetry! Shannon looked at the dumpy little woman beside her. Certainly there was nothing romantic in her sandy hair and pale blue eyes. Her hands on the wheel were red and knotty.

The car swerved around a load of hay and chugged into the main street of the town. A row of miscellaneous automobiles and two old buggies stood in front of the meetinghouse and groups of women hurried along the sidewalk.

They went in together, Shannon and Flossie, and took their seats. Shannon saw the friendly smiles directed toward them. The opening song was one that Shannon had never heard—"For the strength of the hills we bless Thee, our God, our Father's God." For the strength of the hills. Through the window Shannon could see the gap in the mountains where the pioneers came through in the early days. "Thou hast made thy children mighty by the strength of the mountain sod." The music filled the chapel and floated out into the March sunshine.

When it was time to give the lesson, Flossie stood up quietly with no apparent nervousness. Yet her cheeks were flushed and her eyes shining. She held a little sheaf of notes in her hand.

"I noticed the cedar trees today as I was coming to meeting. They are beautiful. At the forks of the road there is a cedar tree taller than most of the others. It grows on a side hill, and you can see its roots spreading out among the rocks."

Cedar trees—almost against her will Shannon loved them— navy blue where they congregate in dark companies on the hillside, raggedly beautiful where they stand in silhouette alone.

Flossie's clear voice continued: "Utah literature is like this cedar tree with its roots in the rocks of this land and its branches reaching skyward. Not mature, a growing thing. Perhaps years will pass before our tree of literature stands superbly grown. The arts are slow of growth. But today, my dear sisters, I want to talk about some examples of Utah literature that I think are worthy of the traditions of our state."

Shannon looked at the women who listened. Some of them she knew. Old Marcia Gudmundson, without chick or child, who lived alone in Cottonwood Lane. Expectancy and eagerness flooded her wrinkled face. She had not been born in the mountain valleys, but she had learned to love them.

Angeline Nagley, whose large family had married and moved away to the city; Angeline, who might have been very lonely indeed. But she did not look lonely. She smiled, and there was a light in her brown eyes. She had come to the meeting to be filled with beauty and inspiration. Shannon saw it in her face.

Flossie spoke of the literature that flowered early in the Utah valleys, the writings of Eliza R. Snow and the other sisters who edited the church magazines. "And the pioneers," said Flossie, "even the leaders who laid the foundations of our inland empire, were poets too. I think you will like these words: 'I found a large room canopied by the sky and walled in by these mountains.' Thus Brigham Young described the Salt Lake Valley, in these very words. They are poetry—earthy poetry."

There was not a sound in the room. Expectantly the women waited. Flossie read again: " 'Their habitation is the munitions of rocks, and they ask no odds of the world, but they are subject to the God who has redeemed this basin.' " Flossie folded a sheet of paper as she explained, "These words were uttered by Daniel H. Wells, who felt deeply the surging pulse of the desert land."

Shannon looked at Trena Olsen, a young woman who had seen little of the world beyond the Fremont. She was married to a farmer and already the mother of a large family. She stared fixedly at Flossie, and her eyes were eager.

Flossie glanced again at her notes. "Since these valleys were first settled, poetry has flowered in the desert; singers have lifted up voices of purity and power. One of our living poets, a woman, wrote these lines. I love them:

> 'Over the knees of the mountains
> Indian summer lies
> Like the golden haze of remembered days
> Over a woman's eyes.' "

For a moment Shannon held her breath, drinking in the beauty of the words. At her side Helga Anderson sighed, "Them's the prettiest words I've heard since my Margaret died. She was a schoolteacher and could read real nice."

Shannon seemed to feel the emotions of all these women. A strange communion seemed to fill the room. She knew that everyone was remembering thoughts too deep for words.

Flossie folded up her notes and sat down. The lines of the closing song assailed Shannon with their lofty melody—"O, ye mountains high where the clear blue sky arches over the vales of the free . . . "

The women lingered at the door. That was a good lesson. We enjoyed it. You did yourself proud, Flossie Nielson. I can live a long time on that. Vaguely Shannon heard their words of praise. Flossie deserved everything they said.

As the car jolted along out into the farmlands again, Shannon sat very still. When they reached the Nielson yard she got out slowly, thoughtfully.

"Flossie, that lesson helped me out so much—so much more than I can say."

"Oh, that's all right, Sister Heath. I haven't much ability, but we all have to do what we can, and I like the meetings."

All her arrogance, all her stupid superiority seemed to have vanished as Shannon walked along a road that meandered pleasantly through Mill Valley. The March wind whipped her cheeks and she heard the roar of the creek as it tumbled boulders and melting ice along its twisted channel. Shannon saw the cedar trees on the hills, and she thought of their roots in the rocks and their branches lifted to the blue.

Vol. 22, no. 3 (Mar. 1935), pp. 139-42.

Vol. 18, no. 5 (May 1931), p. 300.

My Masterpiece

By Elsie C. Carroll

Oft to my soul there come stealing
Sweet visions of consummate art:
A statue, a picture, a poem,
And there awakes in my heart
A longing to carve the fair image,
To color the picture sublime,
To sing for the world the sweet poem:
To create a great masterpiece—mine!

But e'en as I reach for my chisel
Or canvas and brush, or my pen,
And open the door to fancy,
I'm brought to the present again.
An echoing laugh may recall me;
A shrill cry of pain or of fear;
A small, grimy hand on my elbow;
A sweet whispered word in my ear.

And away go my visions a-winging
Back to the fount whence they came;
Before me untouched is my marble,
My canvas is white, my song but a name.
I turn to the needs of my babies
And gazing into their dear eyes,
I thrill with the sense of contentment—
In their future my masterpiece lies.

Vol. 286, no. 6 (June 1928), pp. 311-12.

To Visit the Sick

By Vangie Mae Blair

Louise Farmer leaned back in her chair and glared at her blanket-draped legs propped on the old footstool and felt sorry for herself. She knew it was stupid to feel that way. She was really very lucky, but that didn't seem to make any difference. This was the first time in her life she had been tied down. Even after the birth of each of her five children, she had always been able to get up and do things. Not much, of course, but still she had never felt so physically trapped as she felt now.

"All because of a silly little operation," she said to the vase of wilted daffodils on the table beside her.

Oh, but it wasn't silly, she mentally reminded herself, with a sad shake of her gray head. An operation for her varicose veins had been necessary, important, and for her own good. The doctor had told her that over and over again.

"And now all you will have to do," he had said, "is to keep off your feet and give everything a chance to adjust." As if it was easy to keep off your feet and do nothing. That was the hardest thing in the world, just ask anyone who ever tried it!

She looked around the room in disgust. There was a thin film of dust on her tables, television, and buffet. The rug by the door needed straightening, and all of the flowers were wilted and needed to be thrown away and fresh ones cut and arranged.

It would be so easy, she thought, just to take fifteen minutes and fix it all up.

But she had given her word to the doctor that she would follow, to the letter, his orders of extremely limited movement. All her life she had kept her promises. She was going to keep this one, even if it nearly killed her to do it.

What really topped it off, she thought to herself with a vengeance, was that today was the Sabbath and she couldn't go to her meetings. The benches in the chapel were too hard and much too close together to let her use a footstool to keep her feet up. Oh, she could go and sit on the benches sideways and put her legs up along the bench, but she wasn't going to make a public spectacle of herself at her age.

A squeak and a bang of the front gate caused her to turn and look out of the window. Bobby Johnson was coming up the path, and with the exactness of childhood, he was very carefully stepping only in the center of each and every flagstone.

He jumped up onto the wooden porch and knocked on her door.

"Come in," she called out.

"Hello, Sister Farmer, how are you today?" he said, further wrinkling the rug as he twisted around and firmly shut the door behind him.

"Fine, Bobby," she answered as she watched him walk over to the large, pink wing chair across from her. One of his shoelaces had come untied, and it dragged along the beige linoleum each time he put that foot down.

He perched himself on the edge of the chair and looked at her. A large grin lit up his face and wrinkled his freckled nose. In the glow of such a cute, all-out smile, Louise felt herself smiling back at him.

Bobby is certainly pleased with himself about something, Louise thought, so she asked, "What brings you here? Did your mother send you over for something?"

"No," Bobby said, and started to swing his crossed feet back and forth.

His loose shoelace danced enthusiastically on every down swing. Bobby looked down at his erring lace and bent forward almost double to tie it, bringing him precariously near the edge of the chair, and Louise felt that any minute he would lose whatever balance he had and she would see him fall smack onto the top of his blond head.

He didn't fall, and she sighed with relief as he straightened up, red-faced from his task.

"I went to Sunday School this morning, and my teacher told

us some things that Jesus told us to do on Sunday, and one was to visit the sick and afflict them, so here I am."

After announcing his good works to her, he wiggled back into the large chair, folded his arms, and smiled complacently at her.

Louise smothered a smile with difficulty and said, "Thank you."

"You're welcome."

Louise was at a loss. Just how does one talk to a small boy who comes to visit the sick and afflict them?

From the depths of the chair Bobby looked around the room for a moment and then announced, "Your flowers are dead."

"Yes, Bobby, I know. They need to be thrown out and fresh ones put in their place."

"I'll do it," Bobby said, as he hopped out of the chair and picked up the vase of daffodils from the table beside her and started toward the bouquets on the television and the buffet.

Louise pushed herself forward from the chair and started to protest, but Bobby added, "Jesus said that we're supposed to help people."

She sank back into her chair again. She was plainly in the hands of a doer of good works. After all, things are only things, but people, especially children, are special.

Bobby tucked the vase of daffodils in the crook of his left elbow and hugged a vase of wilted flowers to his chest with his left hand. With his right hand he picked up the vase of hothouse flowers her daughter had left when she had come to clean house and visit last Monday.

Somehow, Bobby made it across the floor and into the kitchen with only one tiny spill on the floor. She heard him dump the water into the sink and pull the flowers out of the vases.

He opened the back door, and she heard a rattling thump as the old flowers hit the garbage can. After the back door was shut again, there was silence for a space and then a small voice said, "I dripped. Where's the mop?"

"Standing up at the side of the house behind the garbage can."

"Oh," he said, as the back door opened and then shut again.

Louise smiled as she heard the scratchy sound of a dry mop

on the kitchen floor. She had always admired Brother and Sister Johnson for the way they were rearing their family; now she admired them even more. There aren't too many little boys who would try to clean up their messes.

There was a pause in the mopping, and a drawer was pulled open. From the sound of the various crashes and clinks, Bobby had pulled out the utensil drawer. He went out the back door, dragging the mop behind him, and firmly shut the door.

In the house all was quiet. Too quiet, Louise thought, as she strained to hear what was going on outside. After what seemed a very long time, Bobby came in at the back door again. Faintly, the smell of lilacs drifted into the front room.

Why, she didn't know the lilacs were blooming! They grew around on the other side of the garage, and she hadn't been able to walk there to see them. She thought, if it hadn't been for Bobby I would have missed the lilacs this year.

Louise heard the splashing of tap water in the sink as Bobby filled the vases. She suddenly thought of something.

"Bobby!"

"What?" he called as he poked his head through the doorway. The water was still running in the sink.

"Could you please put some plates under the vases so the water won't stain the woodwork?"

"Okay," he said, and disappeared.

Louise leaned back in her chair and listened to the small, friendly noises coming from the kitchen.

Some time later, Bobby came in with three plates and put one each on the television, the buffet, and the table by her chair.

When he came into the front room again, his slow steps proclaimed that he was carrying the flowers. This first vase he carefully placed on the television. He stepped back with satisfaction and skipped back into the kitchen.

Louise smiled. The lilacs in the vase looked as if they had been exploded into their present positions. They hung outward and down at alarming angles. Not one of them stood up the least little bit. The stems were too long, and a few of them stayed in only because they had caught on the inside of the sharply curved neck of the vase. It was a pottery vase that her oldest daughter had made in a college ceramics class, and, for the first time, Louise was glad that it was as heavy as lead.

The second vase of flowers Bobby brought in was filled with what she figured were the remaining blooms of her early bulb garden. Miraculously, all of them were standing straight up in the small, white milk-glass vase. When she complimented Bobby on getting them to stay all together so tall, he smiled and said, "I wrapped them together with toilet paper before I put them in the vase. See!" He lifted them up. There was a mass of white sogginess gluing the stems together.

Louise looked from the flowers to Bobby's proudly smiling face.

"That's nice," was all she managed to say.

Satisfied, Bobby put the flowers down and went back for the last vase, whose arrangement could be called "various." Bobby had picked a few of every type of flower he could find, and some weren't even flowers!

There were small yellow flowers from the ditchbank. Their poor little stems were so short that he had balanced their blooms on the edge of the vase, like children hanging their chins over the backs of chairs. A few early blooms, with most of their petals shaken off, stood tall and bare in the center. There were some field daisies and some purple ones that were definitely weeds. Standing aloof in the bunch was a rosebud. Bobby pointed to it proudly and said, "I got that one from my Daddy's bush."

"Bobby, they are all lovely. Thank you very much," she said softly.

The little boy walked carefully back over to the wing chair and sat down. He looked at Louise's legs and asked her, "Do they hurt?"

"No, Bobby, not really."

There was silence for a while.

"Would you like a peanut butter sandwich? I make them good."

"No, thank you."

"You don't have to worry about the bread knife being dirty. I washed all the flower juice off it and dried it real nice. I can cut bread in slices, too. Sometimes they fall into crumby pieces, but most of the time I can cut bread into whole slices. Let me fix you a big fat peanut butter sandwich, okay?"

"I wish you could, Bobby, but the doctor said I'm not supposed to eat things like that until I get up and walk around."

Louise looked at Bobby's face slowly losing its sunshine smile, so she softly added, "But, if you like, you can get me an apple from the refrigerator. You may have one, too."

"I'll get one for you," he said, "but I can't have one because I'm visiting you."

Louise was so busy watching Bobby walking proudly into the kitchen to "help" her that the knock on the front door startled her.

"Come in," she called.

Sister Johnson came in.

"Is Bobby still here? He said he was coming over to visit you, but that was quite a while ago, and I don't want him to tire you out."

"Oh, no, Bobby's not tiring me out. He has been helping me."

Louise gestured with her hand to indicate the new flower arrangements.

Sister Johnson smiled and walked over to the television to balance the lilacs better in their vase. As she turned and poked the flowers, they assumed a more traditional look.

"Yes, he is a big help at times, isn't he?" she asked, smiling.

In the kitchen the water tap was turned on and the splashing sounds meant Bobby was dutifully washing the apple before bringing it in.

The two women looked at each other with understanding.

"Sister Farmer, would you like to go to church with us this evening?"

"I'd love to go. I miss not going to my meetings, but I just can't sit that long on those benches."

"I've got that all figured out," said Sister Johnson. "We can put all of the children in the very back of our station wagon, and you can sit sideways on the seat going there. When we get there, you can use our aluminum chaise lounge, you know, the folding one with green webbing that we bought last summer."

Louise Farmer looked around her front room and thought how nice it would be to get out of the house. She had so missed partaking of the sacrament. If she could sit at the very back . . . "Yes," she said, "I will go with you. Thank you so very much for asking me."

Bobby came out of the kitchen with a bright apple in his hand.

"Hello, Mother. Did you come visiting the sick, too?" he asked.

"That's part of it," Sister Johnson said, smiling, "but mostly I came to get my visiting boy."

"Did I visit you all right?" Bobby asked Louise.

"Yes, Bobby, you visited me just fine. I'm glad you came." She held out her hand, and Bobby took it. "And please come again."

"I will," said Bobby, as he went out the door.

"We'll be by to pick you up fifteen minutes before church," said Sister Johnson, as she closed the door.

Louise looked over her now silent house and smiled at her new flowers. Somehow, the dust on things didn't look quite so bad. The water spot on the floor was slowly drying to a dull un even shadow, but her daughter would clean that up when she came to clean tomorrow.

Let's see, she thought to herself, what can I wear to church?

Then she smiled at herself, because she realized that when a woman starts wondering what she can wear, she is well on the road to recovery.

Vol. 55, no. 4 (Apr. 1968), pp. 272-77.

Pioneers

By Vilate Raile

*They cut desire into short lengths
And fed it to the hungry fires of courage.
Long after, when the flames died,
Molten gold gleamed in the ashes;
They gathered it into bruised palms
And handed it to their children
And their children's children.*

Vol. 28, no. 7 (July 1941), p. 455.

Top: Amy Brown Lyman and members of her general board, 1940.
Bottom: Members of Emmeline B. Wells's general board, December 1918.

Full Measure

By Alberta Huish Christensen

I cannot feel, beloved, that life has failed
To fill the promise of love's early dream:
From that far bluff, how could we two have seen
The long encumbered miles that lay between
Our dawn and dusk—the weary rainless land,
The forest standing ominous and still.
And seeing not, perhaps we asked too much
Of stubborn soil; we chafed that calloused hand
Need clear away the wood-entangled hill.

But oh, in tender memory I hold
Spring dawns that tore asunder our despair,
Piping the mountain shoulders with their gold—
And I shall also take into account
That greater thing than fruitage of the vine;
Richer than heaped-up harvest, in amount—
Our love—which never lost its lucent gleam,
But held us to the pattern of our dream!

Vol. 20, no. 2 (Feb. 1933), p. 76.

Lot's Wife

By Alice Morrey Bailey

She merely turned for one last, stolen look
Before her woman's lingering mind forsook
The home her hands had decked, her smile made
     sweet,
The memories of her children in the street.
A spirit, set on right, must keep front-face
Forever rigid toward the chosen place
And eyes firm-narrowed in the lane of duty.
No wayside resting place and no lush beauty
Should tempt the soul to longing, no lost
Love or glory, and no treasure mete their cost
In nostalgic indecision, not even pity
For a wanton, doomed, and wicked city,
Lest the will be drawn into the sucking blaze,
Consumed to smoke and ash. The backward gaze
Can bend desire, compel the step to halt,
And slowly, slowly turn the heart to salt.

Vol. 38, no. 1 (Jan. 1951), p.11.

No Barren Bough

By Eva Willes Wangsgaard

If you were here I would not mind the whiteness
That threatens path and twig . . . and fading hair.
Your eyes were focused always on the brightness,
Too full of joy to notice boughs were bare.
Snow-laden limbs were only April-burdened
To you who saw in them the petaled vines,
And crystal pasture lands were summer-guerdoned
While siskins threaded scarlet through the pines.

Maturity should be a time for sharing
The blue of vine, the gold of stem and root,
For stripping branches overlate in bearing
And savoring together frosted fruit.
No barren bough I dread nor aging bone,
But withered fruits that I must pluck alone.

Vol. 40, no. 1 (Jan. 1953), p. 15.

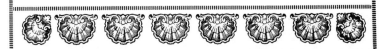

Letter from a Missionary

By Mabel Jones Gabbott

The letter came today; the postman smiled
As if he knew how much it meant to me;
I scanned the date and postmark hurriedly
And then I could not wait. Just like a child
I fairly tore the envelope apart
And read it through. Each closely lettered word
Smiled up at me. Somehow my eyes blurred,
But I could read the message with my heart.

A bit of paper, scratched upon with pen,
And yet it was a vibrant, living thing;
So simply said, "I'm well; don't worry." Then
"With all my love." It made the whole day sing.
So might the saints at Ephesus have waited
Hungrily the word from Paul—like this, belated.

Vol. 47, no. 2 (Feb. 1960), p. 85.

Discrimination

By Olive McHugh

"Your mother is a lovely rose,"
I hear my neighbor say.
She senses not variety;
My Mother is a choice bouquet.

Vol. 27, no. 5 (May 1940), p. 352.

Savior

By Margery S. Stewart

So should I, Lord,
Have hung upon that cross
Which I had fashioned, year on unthinking year,
And felt the nails' torment,
The bitter burn of thirst
And life's slow falling loss.

Save that upon a day thou
Didst quietly take my place,
And died, thorned there, between the thieves,
While angels wept
And earth in darkness mourned
The winnowed stillness of thy holy face.

And on what desolate crosses
Men have died
Rejecting thee, thine offer and thy love. . . .
For who is there to listen
In that dark. . . .
Or be in a lighted instant at his side?
For if the thief could know
He steals to build the beam
On which he will be nailed by and by,
How fiercely he would strive
To find thee past the dark deceptive dream.

The cross, compassionate Lord, was never thine
But composite of all crosses, such as mine.

Vol. 49, no. 4 (Apr. 1962), p. 233.

Narrow Valley
By Zara Sabin

"Is it not too bad?" they said—
When at her service someone read
She had been born, had lived and died
In one small town. Their cheeks, scarce dried,
Were wet again—"To spend her life
As a child, as maid, as mother, wife,
In this narrow valley?"

Narrow valley? Yes, it was true.
The hills were close and steep, the view
Cut off on either side, yet she
Looked at the stars. Instinctively,
Her thoughts reached up to higher things
And knew that more than birds have wings,
Even in a valley.

She heard the first bluebird, or kept
Close vigil where sick child slept;
Baked bread and cakes and sang the while;
Walked her Savior's extra mile;
Then, when her children all were grown,
She died, and had not even known
This was a narrow valley.

Vol. 49, no. 6 (June 1962), p. 439.

Morning by the Sea

By Sylvia Probst Young

On softly rolling water, morning sun
Flecked golden, gently rides toward the land,
And white-fringed wavelets, fingering the shore,
Leave etchings traced in silver on the sand.
Far in the distance, where the blue meets blue,
A ship's hull rises, phantom like . . . the cry
Of soaring seagull breaks the solitude,
In this vast world of sand and sea and sky;
This quiet world where fear and vain regret
Are lost to me—at this lone oceanside,
I walk and feel a power, infinite,
With time eternal—constancy of tide,
And life beginning new at each sunrise—
Beyond the reach of sea I lift my eyes.

Vol. 58, no. 7 (July 1966), p. 557.

Child Asleep

By Christie Lund Coles

Seeing you asleep,
I weep;
Weep for the soft
Gentleness the night
Has laid upon your face,
Like love, like light;
My fingers trace
The way your hair,
Silken and fair,
Falls in soft grace.

Oh, child, so innocent,
So content;
I hear the beat
Of tomorrow's firm,
Relentless feet.
But tonight, sleep.
Sleep sweet.
Oh, child of innocence
And of wonder, sleep.

Vol. 56, no. 1 (Jan. 1969), p. 75.

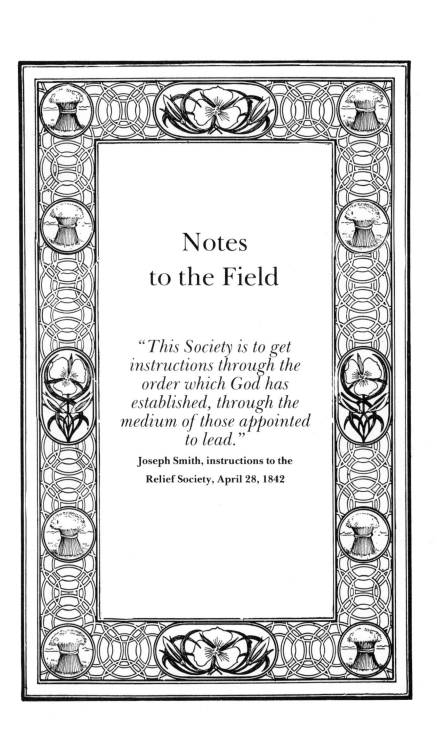

Notes
to the Field

"This Society is to get instructions through the order which God has established, through the medium of those appointed to lead."

Joseph Smith, instructions to the

Relief Society, April 28, 1842

Notes
TO THE FIELD

Vol. 42, no. 4 (Apr. 1955), p. 242.

"Notes to the Field" is a recollection of the testimonies and teachings of Relief Society leaders and the Brethren. Although actually a regular column in which the general board instructed sisters in various aspects of Relief Society work, "Notes to the Field" seems fitting as the name for this section since a major function of the magazine was to send directions and admonitions to leaders and lay Relief Society members alike.

In Relief Society Conference addresses, Relief Society leaders and selected Brethren testified, counseled, instructed, and advised. The selections here present ideas of each Relief Society president who served while the magazine was in circulation.

The editorials sample one of the longest-running features of the magazine. Begun in the 1914 *Relief Society Bulletin*, these articles, usually written by the magazine editor, discussed gospel principles and practices.

Visiting teaching has been a major thrust in Relief Society since its Nauvoo origin. In many respects, it is Relief Society work embodied. Over the years many magazine selections emphasized its importance and necessity. "Where There's a Will" is one of the most charming of these, for it shows a practical side of a spiritual cause.

The Relief Society Building dedication was the fruition of a dream shared by women in both the nineteenth and twentieth centuries. In 1896 General Relief Society President Zina D. H. Young said, "We want to have a house . . . and it should be in the shadow of the temple." From President Belle S. Spafford's announcement in 1947 of plans to construct the home for which

31

women had longed, through the year during which women's individual five dollar contributions mounted to over $550,000, to the dedication services, the building had priority in the magazine.

Members of the Relief Society general board, led by President Belle S. Spafford, at the excavation for the basement and sub-basement of the new Relief Society Building, February 10, 1954.

From Addresses of
General Relief Society Presidents

Emmeline B. Wells   *Clarissa S. Williams*   *Louise Y. Robison*

Amy Brown Lyman   *Belle S. Spafford*

Emmeline B. Wells

I want the sisters to study the scriptures and become familiar with the Bible and the Book of Mormon. Let them be holy books unto you. Take the precepts found there for your guide, for the days are coming when you will sorely need the inspiration which is found in these sacred books. We shall have not only many trials to endure, but we shall be exalted if we endure them faithfully. We must be prepared for what is coming upon the earth. We shall have new revelations as the Lord sees fit to impart them to us. Be obedient to the presiding priesthood wherever you are; sisters, be humble, maintain the truth, follow the majority, for there will always be a majority on the right side in this Church.

Vol. 6, no. 8 (Aug. 1919), p. 439.

Clarissa S. Williams

My dear sisters, I bear to you my testimony, that I know the gospel is true, that I am grateful, more grateful than words can tell, that I have been permitted to live in this day and age of the world when the gospel has been revealed, and that I have been permitted in a humble way to assist in the work of forwarding the gospel here in the world. All I ask is that I may have the Spirit of my Heavenly Father to bless me and to comfort me, to help me that I may have wisdom, that I may have faith, and that I may always have the spirit and the desire to do good to those with whom I am associated. We should love our friends and those with whom we are associated, and as the Savior said, we should love those who hate and despitefully use us. We should bring ourselves to this, my dear sisters, to love all those with whom we labor, whether they are in harmony with us or not. If we could feel that we have the Spirit of our Heavenly Father with us sufficiently that only good would emanate from us, then our associates would know that we are, in very deed, endeavoring to do the will of the Lord and to keep his commandments.

Vol. 9, no. 12 (Dec. 1922), p. 627.

Louise Y. Robison

I have seen strong, brave men who had been separated a while, after they have been in the mission field, and their love at meeting was something beautiful; they would embrace and could hardly be separated from each other, and I have often wondered how such a thing could be, but I have found the secret of it in Relief Society work.

I have been thinking if this Relief Society love could extend all over the world, the Millennium would be here quickly.

There was a little motto that hung in my home when I was a girl. It read, "Welcome the tasks that make you go beyond your ordinary self, if you would grow." If we consider this, it is quite a sermon. Many of our beautiful girls marry and think they are faithful when they give their all in the home with their little people. They are so anxious to be good mothers, so anxious to be good wives, that they feel that they have not time for anything outside. They feel that life is long, and after the children are grown and after they get through with their busy work, they will take up some outside work. It is too bad the young mothers do not know that it is during the time when they are rearing these children that they need the broadening things of [Relief Society] and of the Spirit of the Lord that is obtained in mingling with one another. A woman cannot live entirely by herself, and that includes her children and her husband; to be broad and successful, one writer has said, the only safe way is to have a straight path open from your soul into the great out-doors.

Vol. 8, no. 12 (Oct. 1921), p. 704,

We have met here in the name of Him who came to teach us how to serve, to teach us how to help mankind to a higher level. When we use His methods we not only improve the intellect and aid in cultural development, but there is an actual molecular readjustment. This is Tennyson's meaning when he said: "A great thought strikes along the brain and flushes all the cheek." Thought is the only action the spirit has, and where that thought contemplates spiritual activity and human welfare, it is expressing divinity and becomes entirely and purely creative. Thus the body is uplifted and purified by thinking good thoughts.

Vol. 20, no. 1 (Nov. 1933), p. 634.

Amy Brown Lyman

[Women] have a very acute sense of situations and are often, through this, able to cope successfully with very difficult problems. They have sympathy, imagination, patience, a spontaneous eagerness to help, and a warm good will, all of which are real assets and help them to find their way easily into the hearts of those who suffer. . . .

A picture of the Relief Society in action today is very interesting and enlightening. We see this great army of women attending regular meetings, special classes, and lectures. We see them sewing, quilting, and remodeling clothing, working at canning centers, preserving fruit and vegetables for themselves and others. We see them visiting monthly all the families of the Church —carrying messages of hope and good cheer, making, in addition, special visits to the sick and homebound, and giving many hours of voluntary service to the sick. We find them in homes where death has entered, comforting the bereaved. . . .

Little did the original members of the organization realize, as they walked to and from their meetings in Nauvoo, how great their beloved Society would become in one hundred years. Wisely has it been said that effort can be fully evaluated, not by what the hours, but what the years and the centuries say.

Vol. 31, no. 3 (Mar. 1944), pp. 137-39

Belle S. Spafford

There is within this society a great life-giving element—a spirit which reaches out to women from the eastern shores to the western shores of our own great country, into Mexico and on south to the Latin lands of South America; it reaches into remote villages of Alaska and Canada; it extends into the continents of Europe and Asia, to South Africa and the islands of the sea, binding together women of all nationalities into a great sisterhood, unifying them in purpose and impelling them on to worthy accomplishment. This life-giving spirit is the spirit of the gospel; it is this which makes Relief Society different from other women's organizations the world over. It is this that gives to Relief Society its strength as well as its heart and soul.

Vol. 36, no. 3 (Mar. 1949), p. 149.

Presidency and general board under Belle S. Spafford, 1955.

From Addresses
of
General Authorities

Joseph F. Smith

Heber J. Grant

George Albert Smith

President Joseph F. Smith

On one occasion I visited a distant branch of the Church . . . in the season of the year when malarial fever was prevalent. There were many people of the town . . . where I stopped, who were suffering with malarial fever. The moment I landed from the car, I was invited by the president to go with him and visit the sick. . . . We called on them, visited them, and administered to them. . . . We found, in . . . one instance [a] house where the mother of the little family lay prostrate upon her bed, and her husband distracted for fear she was going to pass away, the little children helpless. [A good sister] came into the room with a basket laden with excellent fruit or food, and other preparations which the children and the family that she was nourishing needed. She took the little children, washed and combed them, and prepared them to sit down to the table. Then she spread food upon the table, and sat the little children around it to eat. Then she turned and administered to the sick mother, and she remained there during, at least, the forepart of the night.

I asked, "How is this done?"

"Well," she said, "our Relief Society is doing it. The Society is providing these things; I am only acting here for the Relief Society, for this evening until midnight, or until sometime in the night, when I will be relieved by another sister, who will bring other things that will be needful during the latter part of the night and for the morning meal."

And I said, "Is this being done throughout the settlement by the Relief Society?"

She said, "Yes."

And I added, "And none are neglected?"

"No, not one, all are provided for. Yes, all are provided for to the best of our ability."

And I said in my heart, God bless the Relief Society.

Vol. 2, no. 1 (Jan. 1915), p. 19.

President Heber J. Grant

My earliest recollection is associated as a child with attending Relief Society meetings. I have even jocularly remarked that I felt I was entitled to be counted as a charter member of the Relief Society, because I had grown up in it. I was an errand boy to distribute the charities of the Society in the Thirteenth Ward. I believe the pleasure I experienced in doing this has had a very great effect upon my life and has impressed me with the force of the saying that, "It is more blessed to give than to receive." I am convinced of that in my own feelings. The work you are doing is a very wonderful and noble work, and I know of no class of people in all the Church who have been more devoted to the work of

God and have labored more diligently to fulfill the obligations and duties devolving on them than our good sisters of our Relief Societies.

Vol. 8, no. 6 (June 1921), p. 338.

Elder George Albert Smith

If the people of this world are to retain their faith in God, it will fall very largely upon the women of this Church to plant this feeling in the hearts of the growing boys and girls and bring into their lives a desire to be worthy of the image to which they have been created.

Vol. 19, no. 12 (Dec. 1932), p. 708.

Hugh B. Brown   *J. Reuben Clark, Jr.*   *Harold B. Lee*

President Hugh B. Brown

[In Relief Society] it is learned that none is so weak as not to bear the relationship of strength to someone weaker still, and that none is so strong as not to bear the relationship of weakness to someone stronger yet.

Much honor is shown to the Priesthood of the Church, and

properly so . . . but when it comes to efficiency, devotion to a cause, self-less service, true religion, hats off to the ladies, God bless them.

Vol. 21, no. 3 (Mar. 1934), p. 133.

President J. Reuben Clark, Jr.

The Lord has chosen us, and chosen you, the Relief Society of The Church of Jesus Christ of Latter-day Saints, to set an example to the world in these hours of stress as to what should be done to care for the poor and the needy, the sick and the afflicted, those in distress. This is your prime duty; all others, as I see it, fade into the distant background at the present time; and your duty must be as was the duty of the Samaritan of old. . . .

And if you will do this you will literally, my brothers and sisters, literally become an ensign to the world; and this Church has never had such glory come to it as will be its glory if you shall fully perform your duties in these respects.

Vol. 23, no. 5 (May 1936), pp. 273-76.

President J. Reuben Clark, Jr.

As you know, at your first meeting you were organized, on March 17th of 1842. During that summer, and until August 31, the Prophet [Joseph Smith] met with the sisters rather frequently. . . .

As I read a little something of the history of those times, I found that the summer of 1842 was one of the most difficult summers for him [Joseph Smith], personally, through which he lived. The infamous Bennett was in Nauvoo stirring up all the trouble he knew how to stir, and he was a good stirrer. The Prophet was driven almost, apparently, to his wit's ends to know what to do. . . .

During this same summer the enemies of the Church, and particularly of the Prophet, in Missouri, sought to involve the

Prophet, in an attempt that was made upon the life of ex-governor Boggs. . . . [Joseph Smith's] time was taken in good part that summer in avoiding the necessity of returning to Missouri. . . .

It was during all of this trouble that he organized this Relief Society, and I felt as I read the account of his talks to them, what he told them, I felt that he had turned to the sisters for the consolation, for the uplift of which he stood in such sad need at that time.

Vol. 36, no. 12 (Dec. 1949), pp. 796-97.

President Harold B. Lee

Largely due to the splendid efforts of the sisters of the Relief Society throughout the stakes and wards, much has been accomplished toward the realization of the purposes of the Church Security Program. Thank the Lord for the Relief Society organization! But, our work has only begun. This coming year we must redouble our efforts, profiting by the mistakes we have made, and add to our success the ultimate triumph of The Church of Jesus Christ of Latter-day Saints in demonstrating to the world its ability to satisfy every need of the human soul.

Vol. 24, no. 3 (Mar. 1937), p. 143.

Vol. 22, no. 8 (Aug. 1935), p. 505.

John A. Widtsoe   *LeGrand Richards*   *David O. McKay*

Elder John A. Widtsoe

"Without the wonderful work of the women, I realize that the Church would have been a failure." So President Heber J. Grant has declared. (*Gospel Standards*, p. 150.) And Paul the Apostle, speaking in an earlier day, said that "neither is the man without the woman, neither the woman without the man, in the Lord." (1 Corinthians 11:11.)

This notable statement implies that woman has done her work well; that she bears joint responsibility with the man in establishing the kingdom of God; and that the work will fail unless both do their duty.

In conformity with this doctrine, full equality has been provided in the Church between man and woman. They are equal in opportunity, privilege, and rights. They have a common destiny, which as free agents they may attain or lose through their own actions.

This makes individuals of man and woman—persons with the right of free agency, with the power of individual decision, with individual opportunity of everlasting joy—for whom all the ordinances of the Gospel are available alike, and whose own actions throughout the eternities, with the loving aid of the Father, will determine individual achievement. There can be no question in the Church about man's rights versus woman's rights. They have the same rights. . . .

If she accepts gladly the glorious gift of motherhood, she

may use whatever time and strength remain in the exercise of her talents as she may desire. She is placed under no limitations. Instead she is encouraged to use her available time in useful pursuits comporting with her natural gifts, her native endowment. The privilege of self-expression belongs to her as to all. . . . And, because of her responsibilities as a rearer of the coming race, she should be carefully, widely, and wisely trained for this important part of her mission in life. . . .

Wherever we touch the life of the Mormon woman, she is found in service, giving unselfishly of herself for the establishment of the kingdom of God. Above all, however, is her service in keeping alive the flame of faith in the souls of her household. Divinely commissioned, in her keeping are the choice spirits who have come to earth to win an earthly body. In her hands lies the future of the race. The mother's teachings outlast the storms of life. Her testimony is never forgotten.

Vol. 30, nos. 6-7 (June-July 1943), pp. 372-75.

Bishop LeGrand Richards

I think you are wonderful. I believe the Lord thinks you are wonderful. . . . I say, "If you want anything done give it to the Relief Society." They never fail. . . .

I would like to say to you sisters who have made contributions to make this [the Relief Society] building possible, that wherever this gospel shall go, throughout all the world, and until the final winding-up scene, this shall stand, the thing that you have done, as a memorial to you, and it shall never be forgotten.

Vol. 36, no. 2 (Feb. 1949), pp. 75-76.

President David O. McKay

Now I don't know that there is any objection to women entering the fields of literature, science, art, social economy, study and progress, and all kinds of learning, or participation in any and all things which contribute to the fulness of her womanhood and increase her upbuilding influence in the world; but I do know that there are three areas or realms in which women's influence should always be felt . . . the realm of home building, . . . the realm of teaching, and . . . the realm of compassionate service.

Vol. 45, no. 12 (Dec. 1958), p. 789.

Spencer W. Kimball   *Mark E. Petersen*   *Joseph Fielding Smith*

Elder Spencer W. Kimball

For you ward teachers or you visiting teachers to accept a responsibility of four, five, six, or seven homes, and leave the people in their spiritual rags and tatters, is without excuse; and when you go into the homes, there should be no "vain babblings" or "swelling words." You go to save souls, and who can tell but that many of the fine, active people in the Church today are active because you were in their homes and gave them a new outlook, a new vision. You pulled back the curtain. You extended their horizons. You gave them something new to contemplate. Maybe they will never tell you about it in all their lives, but you did the work and will be blessed.

Vol. 46, no. 4 (Apr. 1959), p. 215.

Elder Mark E. Petersen

The blessings of the priestly ordinances of the temple are the same for men and women alike. There is no difference. In our marriage, when the sealing blessings are conferred, they are given to the man and the woman equally. The covenants of obedience administered through the gospel again are the same for both men and women. There is no difference. We do not have two standards in the Church. And the promised blessings are likewise the same.

Vol. 57, no. 1 (Jan. 1970), p. 7.

President Joseph Fielding Smith

To be a mother in Israel in the full gospel sense is the highest reward that can come into the life of a woman. This designation has a deep and significant meaning, one that is far more than marrying and bearing children in this life, great and important as that course is.

Vol. 57, no. 12 (Dec. 1970), pp. 883-84.

Relief Society conferences each October drew women to sessions on Temple Square. Top, members enter Assembly Hall in 1950; bottom, sisters mingle between sessions in 1959.

EDITORIAL

Vol. 34, no. 1 (Jan. 1947), p. 50.

Susa Young Gates   Alice L. Reynolds   Mary Connelly Kimball

Belle S. Spafford   Marianne C. Sharp

Editors of the Relief Society Magazine

Susa Y. [Young] Gates

For years we have toiled and joyed together in this glorious work of love and amelioration of suffering which we call Relief Society work. . . .

Wherever our people have gone, there have been Relief Society workers gathering up their means from each other's scanty stores to minister to those who were sick or in want, giving encouragement to the weary and heartsick, while warning the wayward and thoughtless. We have nursed the sick of our people, robed the dying for their last resting-place, fed the hungry, visited the orphan, and succored the needy. This, sisters, is, has been, and ever will be the true spirit and genius of this whole organization. It was inculcated by the Prophet in its beginning and has been reiterated again and again by the leaders of this church who have succeeded him and by the leaders of this organization. We charge you to keep this spirit burning bright in your bosoms.

Vol. 1, no. 1 (Jan. 1914), p. 1. This editorial was printed in the first issue of the *Relief Society Bulletin.*

Alice L. Reynolds

Now, the matter of books. We are very grateful for the libraries that we have, where we can get books to read. However, there are some communities that have not such facilities. I have two suggestions to make. If you are in a community where you have not a single volume of Longfellow or Lowell or Holmes or Whittier, then I believe that this organization, that was organized for relief, should find some way to relieve the situation, even if they have to buy the books. On the other hand, I wonder if we are all aware how frequently we find these poems we are studying, in the school books. Where you have high school students in your homes, you will find that sometimes they are using books on American history and literature. Get hold of the books, borrow them from your children. You will also find that some of the books used in the elementary schools contain a good many of these poems. Do you know that in the pioneer days when the people had not much to eat or much to wear, the wonderful

women who carried on the civilization of this community, somehow or other found things to eat and things to wear. Now, if your
class leaders would go out with the same spirit that the women
went out with when they had to find food and clothing, they
would find a good many books that would answer the purpose.
Let us do our best.

Vol. 10, no. 12 (Dec. 1923), p. 610.

Relief Society Bulletin

Volume 1		Number 1

Issued by the Officers and Directors of the
GENERAL BOARD OF THE RELIEF SOCIETY
1914

HUMAN SERVICE

has come to be a consideration of political parties, or social
organizations, and of educational institutions.

THE RELIEF SOCIETY

has been an instrument of human service for more than half a
century. It ministers to the immediate material wants of the
community. It has been pronounced by many students an
institution for community charity.

THE UTAH AGRICULTURAL COLLEGE

at Logan aims in a very definite way to make each member
of society a more capable producer, a better farmer, housewife, tradesman, agricultural engineer, or business man and
thus aims to eliminate want. Its field of work therefore,
properly co-operates with the work of relief societies in serv-
ing the men and women of the State   While its courses are
distinctly practical, it deals in a broad and fundamental way
with the basic industries of the State. Liberal instruction is
given in the natural and physical sciences, in mathematics,
history, English, economics, literature and languages

The College has been slowly built into an embodiment of
the State's idealism.

NOTE—The Farmers' Round-Up and Housekeepers' Conference convenes at
Logan from January 26 to February 7, 1914. The Utah Dry Farmers' Association.
the State Dairymen's Association, the State Beekeepers' Association, and the
State Poultrymen's Association meet at the College on the same dates.   Reduced
rates are announced over all railroads.

First Press Copy Relief Society Magazine

Mary Connelly Kimball

"Man is that he might have joy."

In a day when people were taught that it was unseemly to be joyous, that the blinds should remain drawn to exclude the sunlight on the Sabbath, that laughter desecrated the Lord's day, and that if one were happy one day he would be miserable the next, came the message, "Man is that he might have joy."

So the restored Gospel emphasizes the importance of being cheerful, of living a happy life. The foundation stone of happiness is trust in God, for calmness, peace, and cheer come to those who trust in the over-ruling providence of the Father. . . .

The loving Father intended we should be happy. A noted doctor has said, "Human life was intended for happiness. If we are not happy, we are using life wrong. Happiness is found in the midst of poverty; happiness has resisted years of unjust misunderstandings. If one is not happy he wrongly blames life; he should scrutinize more deeply his use of it. Parents, teachers, friends, servants, the having or having not, the obtaining or failing, these cannot make us happy or unhappy save as we determine. Just in so far as we succeed in crowding fourteen hours of happiness into our day, . . . have we succeeded in the business of living."

A friend once asked Haydn why his church music was always so full of gladness. He replied, "I cannot make it otherwise. I write according to the thoughts I feel; when I think upon my God, my heart is so full of joy, that the notes leap from my pen; and since God has given me a cheerful heart, it will be pardoned me that I serve him with a cheerful spirit." Commenting on this Van Dyke says, "Pardoned? Nay, it will be praised and rewarded. For God looks with approval and man turns with gratitude to everyone who shows by a cheerful life that religion is a blessing for this world and the next." Happiness is vital to our well-being. The wise man says, "A merry heart doeth good like a medicine." And Christ's reiterated message is, "Be of good cheer." . . .

How glorious is the attitude of George Bernard Shaw, who looks joyously forward. He says, "I want to be thoroughly used up when I die, for the harder I work the more I live. I rejoice in life for its own sake. Life is no 'brief candle' for me. It is a sort of splendid torch, which I have got hold of for the moment, and I want to make it burn as brightly as possible before handing it on to future generations."

Vol. 24, no. 9 (Sept. 1937), p. 594.

Belle S. Spafford

"Let no man seek his own but every man another's wealth." (1 Corinthians 10:24.)

The Master has truly said that it is more blessed to give than to receive, but in giving as in all other activities wisdom is needful. . . .

Many people give to gratify the mastery impulse. Who does not upon occasion like to do the big thing—the generous thing—to be in reality "the Lady Bountiful"? Someone has said giving makes the sublime appeal to the "I am big" which lies deep-rooted within all mankind. At times we give, particularly of our means, to be relieved of further social responsibility. There still remain many, however, whose endless giving is prompted purely by the spirit of the Master—the sincere love of fellowman. But no matter what the deep-seated and underlying motive for giving, be that giving material wealth or service, it builds strength and power—strength to overcome selfishness, to share, to love our neighbor as ourself—and is a source of genuine joy.

Sometimes, in our own selfish unselfishness we give to excess, standing in the way of others enjoying the same satisfactions and development which we so highly prize. Forceful personalities unintentionally but frequently monopolize the giving opportunities within the social group, submerging less aggressive members. When continued over long periods of time, this may result in the individuals so denied having a feeling of inadequacy which affects personality even as lack of physical exercise affects muscular development. . . .

The Savior stands the pattern in giving as in all else. He invariably gave guidance and opportunity that joy and development might come to others.

Vol. 25, no. 8 (Aug. 1938), pp. 554-55.

Vesta P. Crawford

The journals and diaries in which our forefathers recorded their daily experiences, their plans, and their hopes, have now become a choice part of our heritage. There is a wealth of faith, courage, and enduring wisdom revealed in the writings of the men and women who "reared stately columns in the land of Deseret."

One pioneer, who lived through the bitter cold of winter in a dugout, wrote a daily account of hardships and hunger, but he recorded, also, his wealth of faith and joy. "We were always hungry and cold, but we managed to clothe our spirits in fine raiment."

Vol. 34, no. 6 (June 1947), p. 404.

Louise W. Madsen

"Remember the worth of souls is great in the sight of God." (D&C 18:10.) Great is the worth of each individual soul; great is the love of our Heavenly Father for his sons and daughters; great is the gift of free agency which he has given each one. He who uses the gift best becomes self-reliant. He endeavors to fulfill in his own life the Lord's promise of more abundant living to those who seek the higher intellectual and spiritual life.

"Making a living is a necessity, but making a life is a duty, an everlasting blessing," President David O. McKay has said. (*Pathways to Happiness*, p. 1.) Individual effort is required in "making a life," the kind of life which God sent his Son to make possible. No one should be so weak as to depend upon others for the things he should do himself. The weakest of the weak are they who claim that the world, or the government, or the church owes them a living. The strong rely upon themselves. Self-reliance is a virtue when divine guidance is sought. Self-reliance is a virtue when it is based on a conscious effort to achieve self-mastery, to eschew evil. Self-reliance is a virtue if it leads to service and does not become selfishness, nor self-complacency. Self-reliance is a virtue when it is practiced as dependence upon God and oneself to build strength and fortitude.

"Our sufficiency is of God," declared the ancient prophet. (2 Corinthians 3:5.) It was not intended that anyone be completely self-sufficient. Self-reliance is not aloneness. It is more complete trust in the efficacy of keeping the commandments—a more complete reliance upon God's promised blessings. Nor does self-reliance rule out the influence of others, or make it necessary to withdraw from their company. Rather, it means an acceptance of the righteous lessons learned from others' teachings and experiences as part of the necessary preparation to make the fullest use of one's free agency. Self-reliance is by no means self-interest to the exclusion of thoughtful, loving kindness. . . .

"And be not conformed to this world: but be ye transformed by the renewing of your mind. . . ." (Romans 12:2.) Conformity to the things of this world may rob one of the opportunity to renew his mind and refresh his spirit from the things of heaven. The better way lies in conformity to the teachings of the gospel, suiting life to its precepts, and relying on the things one knows to be true. The path of self-reliance should lead one away from the self-indulgence which seems to be prevalent in this day to a more perfect confidence and dependence upon the closeness of God.

Vol. 52, no. 8 (Aug. 1965), pp. 584-85.

Marianne C. Sharp

Changing times bring changing conditions. That is basic to Latter-day Saints who believe in continuous revelation. Changing times have brought the end of the journey to the *Relief Society Magazine*. The times were different when it began in 1914—and that time was the end of the journey for the *Woman's Exponent*. These two women's periodicals have spanned the period from 1872 to 1970. And with 1970 begins a new era in Relief Society when Relief Society members join with the other adult members of the Church in supporting an adult Church magazine [the *Ensign*].

Vol. 57, no. 12 (Dec. 1970), p. 894. This excerpt is from the last issue of the *Relief Society Magazine*.

Where There's a Will

By Donna Durrant Sorensen

When the "Necessity Committee" of sixteen members was formed in Nauvoo, in 1843, to do friendly visiting, this promise was made to them: "The spirit of the Lord will help you in it," and this spirit, through the years since, has moved them to tremendous physical effort under many different conditions. . . .

In Nauvoo the women usually walked from one home to another to gather their reports on the condition of the saints,

Visiting Teaching in a Buggy: Sarah Bartlett Bingham and Evelyn B. Richardson of Vernal, Utah, ready for a trip in a buggy.

and, since that time, walking has undoubtedly been the most usual mode of travel in doing visiting teaching.

Relief Society women in pairs have been assigned to visit each home. A visiting teacher for forty-eight years in one of the southern Utah settlements recalls that she had the same district and the same companion for ten years of that time, and they walked to do their teaching:

> We were having our families then, so often had to take our babies with us. As it would take us the most of a day, we were often treated to homemade root beer in the summer, and in the winter the sisters would ask us in to the fire to warm up. . . . There were no pavements in those days, and we would have to push the baby buggy through the mud. We would often lose our rubbers and really have a hard time to cross the streets. In the summer it was hot and dusty, but, hot or cold, dust or mud, and no matter how busy we were, we always planned to do our teaching on time. And the Lord blessed us in our work.

Until 1943, the visiting teachers accepted contributions for charitable purposes, and one early-day teacher recounts:

> My partner and I would receive contributions of food, soap, clothing, carpet rags, meat, butter, dried fruits, wild berries, etc. We always carried a basket and a sack. The eggs and perishable produce would be put in the basket and the rest in the sack. Sometimes we would receive so many things that we would have to leave them at the homes and go back the next day. If we came into a home where help was needed, we would often stop on our way to help care for the sick, or give a tired mother a helping hand, or take home the unfinished knitting of much-needed stockings. Sometimes, we would return in the evening and sit up with the sick, and at Christmas time we would see that each family had something special for their holiday cheer.

When the people made grain donations and contributions of like nature, the teachers would have to gather them by team and wagon. At a later period most of the contributions consisted of money.

In the colonizing of the various valleys of the Far West, small settlements were established, but still there were isolated families to be visited. In the early period of colonization wagons were used to take the sisters on their visits. Many times this would necessitate the removal of the team for the entire day from the planting and harvesting. As noontime approached, these women would be asked to dinner in one of the homes.

One elderly sister, who is now nearing her ninetieth birthday, lived during her early married life in a farming community of scattered homes. On four different occasions as she and her companion went in a wagon to do their visiting teaching, she was called upon to assist at the birth of a baby. The words of Lucy Smith, the mother of the Prophet Joseph, at the second meeting of the Relief Society, could not have been more literally lived: "We must cherish one another, comfort one another, and watch over one another."

As time went on and people became more prosperous, the wagons used for visiting teaching were replaced by buggies. Two teachers who used a one-horse, light buggy to travel over their district in a scattered vicinity took with them their nursing babies, whom they carried with them into the homes. At one home they visited, they decided the next home would be reached quicker by walking through the fields. As both of their babies were fast asleep, they asked young Mrs. M——, who also had a sleeping baby, if she would mind if they left their babies there with her while they made their next visit. This was agreed upon and the teachers started out. However, they had not gone far before they heard Mrs. M—— calling in a loud voice, "Come quickly, all three babies are awake!"

Wintertime brought hazards to those who traveled long distances to visit. Many times the teachers would start out in good weather only to find themselves in a sudden severe snowstorm far from home. Although they sometimes suffered from the extreme cold and many times arrived home hours late, still they were protected and none lost her life. In midwinter, when the snow was heavy on the ground, they hitched their teams to bobsleighs and thus covered their districts. In one community a team of mules was often used on a wagon in good weather and on a sleigh in the winter.

In many communities the women went horseback to do their teaching. A woman now in her eighties relates that she and a companion, both at the age of nineteen, were chosen to be teachers in a little Latter-day Saint settlement. They rode horseback to do their teaching in the ward, comprising twelve families who lived up and down a creek for the distance of five miles. . . .

A group in one mission field found that the visiting teachers were not able to walk the distances, and so a motor corps of eigh-

Visiting Teaching in an Early Model Ford: Parmelia F. Batty of Vernal, Utah, former stake Relief Society president, and her companion.

teen women was organized, composed of women with cars who could drive. These sisters called for the visiting teachers and drove them to the homes in their districts. In 1931, this group visited from 235 to 265 families each month, and traveled monthly four hundred miles.

The Second World War necessarily brought some curtailment to visiting teaching in many parts of the world. The visiting teachers in one European country, where they had used bicycles to get to the homes, found that they could not purchase new tires. This did not deter them, however, for during the war they used their bicycles without tires and rode on the rims to visit the families. In the United States, however, it was not unusual to find the visiting teachers pooling their supply of gasoline to cover the miles which intervened between families. . . .

Visiting teachers give through their spirits which have warmed, comforted, and blessed those whom they have visited. Their hands have been ready to help, and their hearts have led them into the ways of most helpfulness. . . .

Because they have been willing to exchange the push of circumstances for the pull of a strong worthwhile purpose, the visiting teachers have learned the love of sisterhood, and have been a tremendous force in welding together the individual members of Relief Society into a united whole, and with a consequent building of the kingdom.

Vol. 34, no. 8 (Aug. 1947), pp. 507-13.

The Relief Society Building

Announcement of the Site
President Belle S. Spafford

At the conference held in 1947, we proposed a plan, which you voted upon, whereby our Relief Society women would raise a total of $500,000—or half a million, to be used in the erection of the building. This vast sum of money was to be raised in one year. It was a mammoth undertaking for the sisters, but with characteristic loyalty and zeal, with a spirit of love for Relief Society in their hearts, they went forward to accomplish the task. The blessings of our Heavenly Father were poured out upon us, and just one year, lacking two days, from the time the fund-raising program was launched, we were able to announce in our general conference the full accomplishment of the task we had set ourselves. A total of $554,016 had been contributed to the Building Fund.

Vol. 39, no. 11 (Nov. 1952), p. 717.

Dedicatory Prayer
President David O. McKay

And now, representing them, and by the authority of the Holy Priesthood, we dedicate this building of the Relief Society of The Church of Jesus Christ of Latter-day Saints unto Thee, Holy Father, and set it apart to be used for the purposes for which it has been erected. Accept it, O Lord, and hallow it by Thy

Relief Society President Belle S. Spafford breaks ground for Relief Society Building, October 1, 1953. Looking on are President David O. McKay, President Stephen L Richards, and President J. Reuben Clark, Jr. Amy Brown Lyman, former Relief Society president, is behind Sister Spafford.

protecting influence. Shield it from destructive elements, and may it stand undefaced, a solid structure from foundation to roof, until its every purpose shall have been accomplished.

Vol. 43, no. 12 (Dec. 1956), p. 789. Dedication services were held October 3, 1956.

Loving, United Effort Availeth Much

By Velma N. Simonsen

This conference of October 1956 is of special significance to us. It witnesses the fulfillment of a dream which has persisted in the heart of Relief Society for many, many years—the dream of having a functional and beautiful building of its own. The dream began early in Church history, even in Nauvoo, and continued with the sisters through their forced move from the beautiful city of Nauvoo to the uninviting West, where the sisters continued their work of benevolence, unselfish sharing, and effective service in the Lord's work. . . .

The first day the building was open for inspection two little sisters stood at the entrance to the lounge room, their eyes shining in admiration. One turned to the other and said, "We didn't know our five dollars would buy so much, did we?" Surely loving, united effort availeth much.

Vol. 43, no. 12 (Dec. 1956), pp. 814-15.

Architect's drawing of Relief Society Building appeared in the magazine in March 1948 (vol. 35, no. 3, p. 151).

Relief Society Conference on Temple Square.

Notes
from the Field

*"By union of feeling we
obtain power from God."*

**(Joseph Smith, instructions to the
Relief Society, June 9, 1842)**

Vol. 5, no. 2 (Feb. 1918), p. 100.

More than any other section of the magazine, "Notes from the Field," which ran from January 1915 to December 1970, demonstrated that charity was more than a motto to thousands of Relief Society women. In the throes of depression and war, in the midst of abundance and peace, in struggling branches and burgeoning wards, Relief Society work went forward. Sometimes humorous, sometimes tragic, the accounts in "Notes from the Field" focused attention on the bazaars, visiting teaching, quilting, homemaking, singing mothers, and socials that were so much a part of Relief Society. Vivid accounts of women rallying together under duress poignantly portrayed the heart and soul of Relief Society at its best, and these unsolicited mini-stories of individuals are all the more touching because of the truths they often exemplified.

No Knitting during Meetings

The recent decision of the General Board was that knitting shall not be done during our meeting hours except at the regular work meetings. The inattention which is an accompaniment of active fingers is not polite to the speaker or class teacher, nor does it permit the members to get the most out of their lesson work. Our sisters will have plenty of time at home and in work meetings to do all the knitting for which they can obtain yarn and thus assist the Red Cross cause.

Vol. 5, no. 2 (Feb. 1918), p. 101.

Cottonwood Stake

The Cottonwood Stake held a very successful bazaar. . . . A children's dance was given in the afternoon on the second day, free of charge, and a baby show was conducted at which fifty-two babies under one year were exhibited. Each baby received a small prize, and the winner a special prize. The proceeds from the stake and wards amounted to near $1,000, and will be used for charity.

Vol. 3, no. 11 (Nov. 1916), p. 634.

Vol. 11, no. 9 (Sept. 1924), p. 455.

Northern States Mission

When twelve thousand earnest Red Cross workers marched down Michigan Boulevard, Chicago, and into the famous U.S. War Exposition, in honor of their national chairman, a company which attracted considerable attention was Auxiliary 615, representing the National Women's Relief Society of Chicago.

The Northern States Mission has twenty-four other Relief Society auxiliaries, all actively engaged in Red Cross work.

Vol. 6, no. 1 (Feb. 1919), pp. 102-3.

Red Cross Work in the Relief Society

A plan of co-operation has been outlined whereby Relief Society members who desire to assist the Red Cross may do so in Relief Society groups and be known as Relief Society Red Cross workers. By this arrangement the identity of the Relief Society will be maintained.

The General Board advises that while rendering this additional service, Relief Society workers do not neglect in any way the regular relief work of the Society.

Vol. 4, no. 8 (Aug. 1917), p. 430.

Sandwich Islands [Hawaii]

A Relief Society has recently been organized in Wailuku, Maui, with twenty-seven members, who are meeting regularly. In addition, these members are meeting Thursdays to do Red Cross work.

Vol. 6, no. 1 (Feb. 1919), p. 103.

Summit Stake

On October 30, 1923, at Kamas Ward, in the Summit Stake, a very successful social was given by the officers of the Relief Society, in honor of the thirteenth anniversary of the dedication of the Relief Society building of that ward. . . .

The Relief Society building was started sixteen years ago and was completed in about two and one-half years, and is valued at $2,200. The society has just completed a cement walk on the entire south side of the lot, which is one half a city block, and has also put in a water hydrant.

Vol. 11, no. 3 (Mar. 1924), p. 145.

Utah Stake

1930 was also the 88th anniversary of the organization of the Relief Society. At the Utah Stake celebration there was . . . a "gala" afternoon. . . . The stunt program followed on scheduled time and with unusual pep:

1. Silent picture revealed Joseph Smith giving the keys, and the growth of the work up to date, culminating in motherhood glorified through Relief Society work.

2. Scotch Lassies with harmonica band.

3. Eliza R. Snow writing "Oh My Father."

4. Misfortunes of a Relief Society sister taking her Sunday eggs to "Help the cause along."

5. Story told in rhyme and acted by 21 sisters, telling of overcoming difficulties in Relief Society work on the way to their goal—"success."

6. An officers' meeting 100 years hence. Imagination was not cramped. The judges, believing in a forward look, gave decision here.

7. Two sisters of 30 years' experience led out. "Love to serve" was beautifully portrayed.

8. "Health and Beauty," 10 years hence through Social Activity.

9. "The Last Quilting," where all finally yielded to these "new fangled ideas.". . .

Eighty-eight years of growth finds the Spirit of Truth (theology), Culture (literature), Progress (special activity), Service (Social Service), and Peace (work of visiting teachers), all smiling as multitudes pluck fruit from the branches of the Relief Society tree. The most luscious fruit of all their plucking is the gift of Motherhood.

Vol. 17, no. 9 (Sept. 1930), pp. 504-5.

Northern States Mission

While the sisters have been brave and kept their organization together, it has been impossible for them to do as much in a financial way as they would like to do. However, the spirit has been very brave and fine. There is a new organization at West Frankfort, Illinois. These sisters are living in the Illinois mining district, where most or all the men are out of work. The president, Sister Allie Y. Pond, made a call for old clothing, and the response was wonderful. Six boxes of good clothing were sent. . . .

Word came that a woman out away from any Relief Society was destitute, and there were six little children in the family who could not go to school because of lack of clothing. When the president reported this to the Relief Society, within a few days two large boxes of clothing were on their way to supply their needs. This sister, after three weeks, reported that she had sewed night and day, and now all her children were ready for school, and her gratitude was unbounded. . . .

All of the Relief Societies are busy in preparation of programs for the 17th of March. Really and truly Relief Society work is wonderful.

Vol. 18, no. 4 (Apr. 1931), p. 225.

Rigby Stake

The above picture is characteristic of the faith and "stick-to-it-iveness" of the Relief Society sisters of the Bybee Ward, Rigby Stake. When the roads are impassable for autos, and impossible for sleighs, the meetings continue with a large attendance, the sisters coming in what they christened "The Gospel Wagon."

Vol. 19, no. 8 (Aug. 1932), p. 478.

French-Polynesian Mission Relief Society Bazaar

The small articles were woven hats, bags, mats, fans, carvings, doilies, clothing, pillows and pillowcases, grass skirts, and some very artistic shell vases. Fifty very beautiful tifaifai (bed covers, with applique or crazy-quilt patterns) were also sold. The basketball court was divided into booths, with the name of each island in front, so that the customers could see from which island they were buying the articles. We were very proud to display a tifaifai which had won first prize in the territory-wide contest last July, and also the one which had taken first place for originality of design. . . .

The day was very rewarding, and the sisters have never had such a successful sale.

Vol. 49, no. 8 (Aug. 1962), p. 609.

British Mission

The presidency of the Relief Society in Edinburgh . . . sent the following report, dated December 15, 1939, of the conduct of Relief Society work since the beginning of the war and consequent withdrawal of missionaries:

"We decided to put away all the dainty work that was being done for a sale of work at Christmas to help our funds. As we did in the last war, we decided to work for the hospitals and for the Red Cross, which has given us much work and also a box for collections. We tried meeting in daylight, but as we all have to work it was not convenient, and we now meet at the hall at 6:30. The streets are very dark, shops shut at six, and cars trundle along dim and rather ghostly. Owing to the sandbags against the buildings, every sound seems to develop an echo. The cars sound like gunfire at certain points. The hoot of a ship at sea or a railway engine is often taken for the air raid warning, which by the way is a terrifying wail.

"We in Edinburgh have many non-members in our work party, all very keen to help and willing to take part in our program on open night. We need your prayers that we along with all our members in other nations may keep the faith, and that our Father in his love may shorten these days."

Vol. 27, no. 4 (Apr. 1940), pp. 277-78.

Netherlands Mission

Franklin J. Murdock, Church mission secretary and former president of the Netherlands Mission, sent the following report: "I had the pleasure yesterday of reading a letter direct from the little war-torn country of Holland. It is the first direct information which we have received relative to conditions there since the invasion of that little country by Germany. The letter was written by Sister Zippro, who is president of the Relief Society.

". . . Just as soon as the two armies had concluded . . . firing, Sister Zippro left her little family in Amsterdam with her husband and bicycled from Amsterdam to Rotterdam, a distance of sixty miles. It took nine hours to make the trip. . . .

"The terrible destruction of life and property was abundantly exhibited on every hand. She says she has never seen so many men marching, so many tanks, airplanes, and tractors, which caused a tremendous destruction of life. She found many families in Rotterdam who had had their homes, furniture, and all earthly belongings completely destroyed and had gone to live with other members temporarily. The old hall in Rotterdam had been completely destroyed, but the new chapel overmass was still intact, and the members were planning to hold Sunday School there."

Vol. 27, no. 9 (Sept. 1940), p. 626.

East German Mission, Leipzig District

Sister Lena Glaus, president, East German Mission Relief Society, reports the many problems and opportunities for service in the East German Mission: "We think our mission is the best mission in the whole Church. Do you know why? Because no other mission has as many problems as we have. Our mission is made up of ten districts. . . . These women are like our pioneers of old—they can 'take it,' and they are true to the core. I am sincerely thankful for the opportunity I have of laboring here in Germany with these fine people."

Vol. 39, no. 6 (June 1952), p. 409.

British Mission, Welsh District

Cardiff Branch Relief Society Singing Mothers and Their Daughters Who Furnished the Music for District Conference

This Relief Society, organized for only a year, has grown steadily in cultural, relief, and spiritual activities. From two members, it has grown to twenty active sisters who are in great demand as a chorus at all district functions.

Vol. 39, no. 7 (July 1952), p. 471.

Wasatch Stake (Utah)

Midway First Ward Visiting Teachers Make a One-Hundred Per Cent Record for Forty-one Years

Jennie Johnson, former president, Midway First Ward Relief Society, reports that the . . . picture is a representative group of visiting teachers of that ward who have helped to establish and maintain a remarkable record. . . . The sisters set as their goal a one-hundred per cent record for the year. For seven years, in the face of untold reverses, they worked for this achievement. The ward is a rural community, and the families somewhat scattered. . . . At certain seasons of the year the roads are practically impassable, and the sisters at times had to depend only on horse or foot power to reach their destinations. Finally, in 1913, they were able to establish their hoped-for record. They never again relaxed their standard, and those who followed them in leadership accepted this standard as a sacred trust. . . . Many of the sisters who helped to establish and maintain this record are now deceased, but the daughters, granddaughters, and, in some cases,

the great-granddaughters of these noble women faithfully carry
on the work.

Vol. 42, no. 6 (June 1955), pp. 398-99.

Emily Chadwick Zaugg Makes Many Quilts

Emily Chadwick Zaugg, West Point, Utah, has made many
quilts . . . for many people and for many homes, for gifts to
members of her family and for Relief Society bazaars.

Mrs. Zaugg, now eighty-five years old, is the mother of twelve
living children. . . . As a young mother of six children she carried
the responsibility of the family, while her husband served on a
two-year mission. While living in LeGrande, Oregon, Mrs.
Zaugg helped to operate a family dairy, churning three gallons
of cream at a time and molding the butter into two-pound "pats."
She read the *Relief Society Magazine* while turning the churn. She
was president of Relief Society in the Mountain Glenn Ward in
Oregon for seventeen years, and during that time her thirteenth
child was born. Three years later her husband was called on
another mission. . . . In 1948, she became the Relief Society work
meeting leader and has had charge of the quilt-making projects.

Vol. 43, no. 6 (June 1956), p. 397.

Scottish-Irish Mission

Scottish-Irish Mission Relief Society Float Made for the Lord Mayor's Parade, Belfast, Ireland, May 13, 1961

. . . Nada R. Brockbank, president, Scottish-Irish Mission Relief Society, sends the following excerpt from the *Belfast Telegraph* newspaper report of this entry in the Lord Mayor's parade, titled: "It's Still Tough Going West."

"It's tough, traveling west in a covered wagon—whether you are heading for Salt Lake City or for the Ormeau Embankment.

"The hazards of a journey from Dundonald were fully experienced by the Relief Society of Ireland's float. . . . The float—a covered wagon complete with pioneer family, fire, pots, cradle, butterchurn, and two lads with rifles to ensure 'safety in the home'—was making good progress . . . when disaster struck.

"A wheel sheared off. With true pioneer spirit, they set about repairing it. Even though it turned out to be a major engineering task needing expert help, the wagon was soon rolling again.

"But it arrived five minutes too late for the judging—and all three judges commented that they would have had no hesitation in awarding it a major prize.

"It happens like that—traveling west!"

Vol. 49, no. 2 (Feb. 1962), p. 129.

Santaquin–Tintic Stake, Utah

Bertha Dickinson (left), and Melvina Jolley (right) of Santaquin–Tintic Stake, Utah, have served a total of more than one hundred years as visiting teachers.

Vol. 52, no. 4 (Apr. 1965), p. 289.

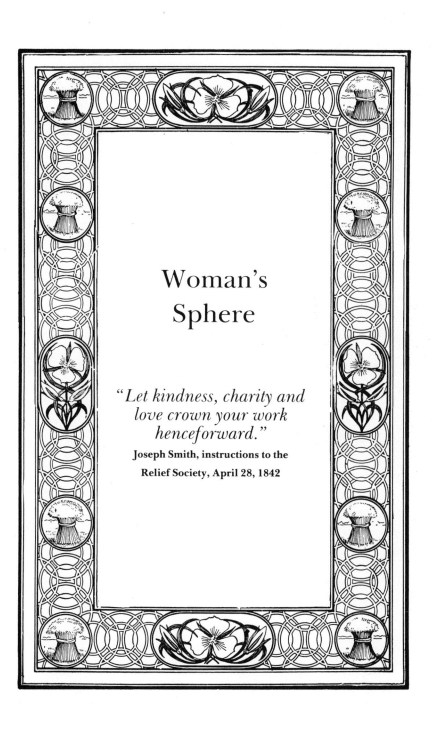

Woman's Sphere

"Let kindness, charity and love crown your work henceforward."

Joseph Smith, instructions to the

Relief Society, April 28, 1842

Woman's Sphere

Vol. 35, no. 3 (Mar. 1948), p. 181.

"Woman's sphere, hitherto confined expressly within the four walls of her home, was now to be limited only by the confines of the Kingdom of God itself." So wrote Susa Young Gates. (*Relief Society Magazine,* March 1919, p. 139.) The Society was to affect all areas of a woman's life, for, as Joseph Smith himself had said, "As you increase in goodness, let your hearts expand [and] . . . be enlarged towards others." (*Relief Society Magazine,* March 1915, p. 94.)

And Relief Society did expand many a woman's sphere. The name of this section, a column title in the latter years of the magazine, aptly expresses its contents; included here are selections that speak to numerous areas in which women make positive contributions.

Relief Society women felt it a duty—even a privilege—to contribute by making their world at home and in the community a better place. They struggled against disease, fought for the vote, sponsored health and sanitation legislation, joined the Red Cross, and shared carloads of clothing with war-torn Europe.

While Mormon women looked forward in their community activities, they also looked back. Stories of yesterday's women were told in a biographical series based on the lives of well-known Relief Society leaders. In subsequent years the magazine added tributes to little-known women whose private lives were filled with faith and courage. These short vignettes share experiences that still strengthen modern generations of Mormon women.

In her efforts to let "kindness, charity and love" crown her work at home, the Relief Society member constantly looked for new and better ways to do things, from improving her health and grooming, to trying a new recipe in the kitchen, to finding innovative ways to accomplish ever-present household tasks. How-to homemaking tips were found in every issue of the magazine. In these practical hints the spirit of the times was evident.

Dedication to principles of providence and a love of culture and children mark many magazine features. Committed, thoughtful women often wrote of their insights and inspirations on subjects ranging from gardening to dealing with stress, showing clearly that a woman's sphere is indeed limitless.

Vol. 5, no. 1 (Jan. 1918), p. 35.

Wheat to Allies

This spring, in April, there were in the elevators belonging to the "Mormon" women of Utah and other adjacent Western States 205,518 bushels of first-class milling wheat. Last month these devoted women felt that the time had come for them to use their precious savings of more than sixty years. Through the presidency of the "Mormon" Church every pound of this wheat was tendered to and accepted by the United States Food Administration for the use of the starving women and children among our allies, and for the use of our soldiers and sailors in the Army and Navy of the United States. . . .

Mr. Hoover's letter follows:

Washington, D.C., June 3, 1918
. . . The recent action of the women of the Church of Jesus Christ of Latter-day Saints, in Utah, in releasing wheat and flour for the use of our allies and our own soldiers abroad is so commendable that I wish to drop you this line merely to assure you of my appreciation of this service performed by the church.

It has given me pleasure to write about this matter to Joseph F. Smith, Anthon H. Lund, and C. W. Penrose, first presidency, Church of Jesus Christ of Latter-day Saints, and to assure them of the renewed courage we get from this generous act, both because it yields a substantial addition of food sorely needed by our hard-pressed allies and also because the example is felt far outside the field of its immediate application.

Yours, faithfully,
HERBERT HOOVER

Vol. 6, no. 10 (October 1919), p. 566.

Relief Society Wheat Field, Moulton, Idaho.

Note Returned to a Utah Girl from Army Front

I want to thank you for the socks you knit.
But sorry to say they do not fit.
Wear one for a scarf and one for a mitt.
Where in the world did you learn to knit?
Vol. 5, no. 1 (Jan. 1918), p. 29.

Relief Society Clothing Drive
for Central Europe

Recently the Relief Society, supported by the First Presidency, issued a call for clothing to supply the needs of the people in central Europe, principally in the German Mission. With something of the rapidity that follows the touch of an electric button, each stake got to work to collect shoes and clothing and bedding. The result was little less than marvelous. . . .

The generosity of the Latter-day Saints has been tested many times, during and since the war, always with surprising results. The recent call for clothing, which brought together two large rooms full of clothes, both old and new, from which three carloads have already been shipped, is no exception to the rule.

The response throughout the Church has been deeply gratifying, and is another evidence of what can be done by an association as completely organized as the Relief Society, and equipped with women whose ability to lead and execute has again made itself manifest in this latest project, as in many others, in times past.

Vol. 11, no. 2 (Feb. 1924), p. 65.

From the European Mission

Very interesting letters have been received at Relief Society headquarters from the European Mission, expressing appreciation and thanks for the carloads of clothing sent to this mission during the past winter. . . . Our readers will be interested in the letter from President and Mrs. [David O.] McKay, which we print in full:

"*Dear Brethren:* Fourteen crates of shoes and seventy-two bales of clothing have been delivered here at Durham House free of charge, excepting dock charges, customs duties, etc., which we may probably have refunded.

"The Leyland Steamship Line, part of the White Star Steamship Line, brought the freight gratuitously from New York to Liverpool, and the Canadian Pacific Railway Company, also gratuitously furnished drays and draymen to cart the 21,640 pounds from the docks to Edge Lane.

"In behalf of the Elders and Saints of the British Mission permit me to thank you and, through you, all those who have in any way contributed, either of their time or means, to this magnificent gift to the poor in this land. Only those who have had to help handle these scores of two-hundred-weight bales and from two hundred to nine hundred pound crates can realize what a stupendous undertaking it was to ship three car loads of shoes, clothing, etc., from Salt Lake City to Europe.

"All praise to the Relief Society and to all other members of the Church and friends who have participated in this philanthropic work. . . .

" 'By their fruits ye shall know them.'
        "Affectionately yours,
        (Signed) David O. McKay."

Vol. 11, no. 8 (Aug. 1924), pp. 420-21.

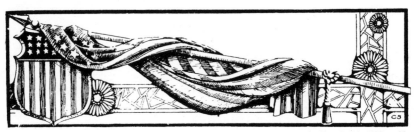

Vol. 19, no. 2 (Feb. 1932), p. 96.

Mothers in Israel: The Nauvoo Battle

By Mary Ann Stearns Winters

Note.—We give this month a vivid picture of conditions in Nauvoo, at the time of the Exodus, that in striking simplicity and pellucid description might well be a companion piece of Colonel Thomas L. Kane's masterpiece on the same subject.

Our supply of provisions was getting low, but the quails came, and Ami Shumway, son of Sister William Pratt, went out to help capture them, and we girls took them to the river, a few feet distant, and picked and dressed them ready for use. When the good people of St. Louis heard the condition the Saints were in, they sent a boat-load of provisions to relieve their wants. The people were counted, and given so many pounds each, according to the number of their family. There was flour and corn meal, from which to take your choice, sugar and coffee, rice, dried apples and bacon.

My baby brother, Moroni, not quite two years old, was sick with chills, so it fell to my lot to go for our share of the supplies. The water was low, and the boat could not get above Montrose, so all had to go there for their rations. I, in company with others, went down and received ours, dealt out from the bow of the boat, and joyfully took it—shall I say *home* with me? Yes, for it is always home where Mother is. . . .

Little Martha Pratt, four years old, had suffered with chills for a number of weeks, and though her condition did not seem alarming, still she did not get better, and one morning her mother noticed a change—she continued to grow worse all day, and when Sister Pratt took her in her arms to prepare her for the night she could see that the end was near, and in a short time she passed peacefully away. But oh, the agony of that loving mother's heart, to lose her beautiful, blue-eyed darling, in such a place and at such a time, and she cried out, "Oh, I can never leave her in this lonely place." But Mother tried to comfort her by telling her that perhaps we could take her over to Nauvoo and lay her by the side of *our* loved ones and then it would not seem so terrible. So in the morning Brother Pratt went over to see if it could be accomplished, and found there was nothing to hinder—the city was as still as death, and the few persons seen on the streets moved around as if at a funeral. A little red pine coffin was procured at Montrose and about one o'clock we started on our mournful journey. Mother could not leave her sick baby, so I was sent to tell them where the graves were, and show them the place Mother thought best for their little one to be buried.

During the summer, Mother had, in anticipation of our leaving the home, obtained stones from the Temple yard, and now she had the initials cut on them, and then after making a chart of the graves from the corner of the house, Brother Silcox dug down at the head of each grave and placed the stones down almost to the coffins, then covered all over and dug up the rose trees we had planted there, and smoothed off the ground, and no stranger could tell where they were.

Vol. 4, no. 2 (Feb. 1917), pp. 77-82.

Mothers in Israel

By Margaret McIntire Burgess

My mother's name was Anna P. McIntire, and she belonged to the first Relief Society that was organized in the Church, the Prophet Joseph Smith's wife Emma being the president.

I must now tell you something of my childish personal incidents at Nauvoo, our place being two blocks above the Nauvoo Mansion. We were close neighbors to the Prophet's family, and very intimate, too. The Prophet was often in our home for short visits. One morning he came in and he noticed I had a piece of flannel around my throat. He inquired if my throat was sore. Mother told him it was, and she was afraid it was the mumps. He called me to him, took me upon his lap, took the flannel off, and asked Mother for the oil. He anointed my throat with the oil and then he administered to me. I knew I was well, as I got down from his lap, after which I felt no more sore throat—another proof of his tender, loving heart.

One morning as we were on our way to school, my brother and I were forced to walk in some very muddy places as it had rained the previous night. The school was down near the river and there was one very bad place we had to go through where we got stuck fast, and I began to cry, as did my little brother. I thought I would surely never get out, but on looking up, we saw the Prophet coming right for us. The crying soon ceased. He carried me out first and then my brother. He took his handkerchief out of his pocket, wiped the tears from our eyes, and cleaned the mud off our shoes, all the time speaking comforting words to us, sending us on our way rejoicing, at the same time pointing out a safer way to get to the schoolhouse. Oh, our beloved Prophet, how deep were his sympathies and how his kind heart yearned to do good.

Now, let me tell you another incident before I stop. My mother had twin baby girls, and Aunt Emma, as we called her, (the Prophet's wife) had been confined, and her babe had died; soon after the birth the Prophet came in one morning and said, "Sister McIntire, I have come to borrow one of your babies," and Mother exclaimed, "Why, Brother Joseph, what do you want with one of my babies?" "Well," he replied, "I want one of them for my wife to comfort her only for a time." He talked with Mother a while and she finally told him he could have one baby through the daytime if he would bring it back nights, so the bargain was made and the Prophet smiled with gratitude.

The twins were so much alike they could scarcely be told apart, but, of course, Mother knew their dispositions were not alike—one was a quick little thing and the other one was mild. My mother would set them in the double cradle, made high at each end and low in the middle, and give each some playthings, and the quick one would take all the things away from the mild one. They were dressed exactly alike.

One morning when the Prophet came for the baby, Mother reached him the other baby. He took it and looked at it, kissed it and handed it back and said, "Not my little Mary," so Mother reached him little Mary. He had always taken the little mild one —her name was Mary and the other one was Sarah.

The Prophet would always bring the baby up himself at night. One night he did not come as usual and Mother went down and found the baby was crying. Brother Joseph was sitting by the fire trotting it. He had it wrapped up in a little silk quilt, preparatory to starting out with it. When Mother went in it reached its hands to her. When she took it, the baby soon was still. When Mother started back, the Prophet took the baby from her and walked up home with her. When Aunt Emma's health returned, our baby came home to stay. When she was able to walk she came often to see baby Mary, as our home was only two blocks from the Mansion.

Vol. 5, no. 1 (Jan. 1918), pp. 14-15.

Vol. 5, no. 1 (Jan. 1918), p. 43.

Mrs. S[usa] Y[oung] Gates'
Popular Fruit Cake

For Two Large Cakes.
The inside crumbs of 2 5-cent loaves of white bread.
2 lbs. Blue Ribbon raisins.
2 lbs. seedless raisins.
1 lb. chopped walnuts, more or less.
1 lb. butter. If suet is used this recipe makes a plum pudding.
2 scant lbs. sugar.
2 heaping teaspoons cinnamon.
1 nutmeg.
3 tablespoons essence of lemon.
8 eggs, beaten separately.
1 qt. sour milk and
1 even teaspoon soda or
1½ pt. sweet milk, and
2 teaspoons yeast powder.
1 pt. flour with soda or yeast powder sifted in.

Cream butter and sugar, add creamed yolks of eggs, then whites and milk; sift the flour in the raisins and nuts, add bread crumbs to milk, sugar and eggs. At the last add the floured fruit; put at once into pans and bake in a moderate oven over three hours.

Vol. 5, no. 1 (Jan. 1918), p. 44.

Ten Conservation Commandments

1. We can have a few more meatless days—that is obligatory on most of us.

2. We can substitute corn meal, rye, rice and oatmeal at least two days a week for ourselves and families.

3. We can save every scrap of good food and use it for our own human needs rather than throwing it in the garbage pails.

4. We can practice the doctrine of the clean plate.

5. We can preserve and take care of every bit of food stuff that we now possess against a time of greater need which is coming.

6. We can cease drinking milk as adults and give the milk to the children or sell it to the creameries.

7. We can mend our old clothing and wear it as long as it is respectable.

8. We can go back to the old-fashioned industries of soap-making and rag-weaving.

9. We can wear mended shoes and keep the children's shoes well greased against wear and cold weather.

10. We can keep cheerful and realize that these are the last days, that the judgments will affect the House of Israel quite as much as it will the nations of the earth for a time at least.

Vol. 5, no. 9 (Sept. 1918), p. 519.

Hoover Cake

2 cups hot water.   *2 cups brown sugar.*
1 1/2 teaspoonful cinnamon. *4 tablespoonfuls shortening.*
1/2 teaspoonful cloves.

Boil these ingredients for five minutes; let cool and add 3 cups of barley or wheat flour, 1 cup of raisins and 1 teaspoonful of soda. Put into a well greased pan and bake for three-quarters of an hour in a medium oven.

Vol. 5, no. 9 (Sept. 1918), p. 519.

An Adequate Daily Diet
and Wartime Menus
By Edna K. Ward

The importance of food and its proper preparation is brought to the attention of every homemaker by the exigencies of total war which have been forced upon us. We want to "make America strong," but a nation is made strong only as its people are strong and healthy.

Each mother and homemaker is largely responsible for the health of her family; she must plan healthful meals, she must buy the food which is to constitute those meals, and now when help is scarce, she has the added responsibility of preparing that food to save important food values.

To plan and prepare "wartime menus" is a challenge to every homemaker. It is her contribution to the war effort, and it is an important contribution. . . .

In planning meals, particular attention should be given to what are termed *protective foods*, protective because they contain elements known to be essential to good health.

Vol. 30, no. 4 (Apr. 1943), p. 286.

Cheese Pudding

5 slices whole wheat bread
2 tablespoons butter
1 cup grated cheese
1/2 tablespoon mustard

2 tablespoons chopped onion
1/2 cup parsley (chopped)
3 eggs (beaten)
2 cups milk

Spread bread with butter and cut in cubes. Place in baking dish, add cheese, mustard, onion and parsley. Add warmed milk to eggs and pour over bread mixture. Bake 350° for 30-40 minutes.

This is a good meat substitute and contains a long list of protective foods such as milk, eggs, cheese, parsley and whole wheat bread.

Vol. 30, no. 4 (Apr. 1943), p. 290.

Indestructibility of Matter

By Helen Hinckley

You remember, of course, that a falling apple introduced the theory of gravity, and that a dancing tea-kettle lid was the father of the steam engine. I only mention this to show how very ordinary things bring about the discovery of the greatest scientific truths.

Although no textbook mentions her name, my mother was, I am sure, one of the pioneers in the field of the Indestructibility of Matter.

Mother bought that blue serge suit way back in 1912. "It looks durable," she commented as she ran a practiced finger across the twill. "It looks as if it would hold up."

For two years she wore the suit with diminishing pride. The box-pleated peplum and the elaborately braided coattail had lost their style after two springs and two falls. I was rather disappointed when she decided to make it over for my older sister. Of course I knew that someday I would have my turn at it, but I had hoped to get it in the first reincarnation.

Mary was in the sixth grade and felt very smart in a real suit with a frilled and tucked voile shirtwaist. After two years the suit had not changed at all, but Mary had. Her hands dropped a surprising distance below the coat sleeves, and her legs were out at the bottom almost up to the knees.

I began to look through the fashion sheets. Surely my winter wardrobe would be constructed of blue serge—but no! Mary was to go to high school now and she must not go without plenty of "changes." The advisability of a strip of velveteen on the bottom to cover up knobby knees was discussed but Mother rejected it as being a too apparent revival. Instead she dropped the skirt to the bottom of the jacket, finished the sleeves with long fitted cuffs salvaged from the superfluous coattail, and bought a patent leather belt. The belt was, I believe, the most beautiful thing that I have ever seen. It was at least four inches wide, bright green in color, and marvelously shiny. It and the swanky green tie would be salvation for any frock.

Two years more I waited before I came into my inheritance. I had grown outward, not upward, and the waist of the blue dress would not stretch over my bulgy form. The cloth was still sound as new, and initiative soon found a way. The pleated peplum was taken from a mothproof chest. This was elongated with strips from skirt number one, and a yoke was made from the former waist. Mother called the result a Mary Pickford dress. She could have truthfully called it a Mother Hubbard but I wouldn't have worn it with that name. A shiny belt was denied me because it would make me look "like a pudding bag, tied in the middle," but a beautiful collar of eyelet embroidery satisfied my craving for the artistic.

When I entered high school Mother folded the serge regretfully and put it away. It was rather glistening now, but only the back panel was threadbare. A few weeks went by and I "made" the girls' baseball team. We were far too modest to run around in bloomers or shorts so we decided on blue skirts and white middies. My middy was new—my skirt was constructed from the everlasting serge, neatly washed, pressed, turned, and re-pleated.

The last time I remember seeing the suit in actual use was in combination with some flannel that Mother had bought from a remnant counter and found inadequate to cover my younger sister. The red really looked very smart with its wide bands of good serge.

A visit from my grandmother saved the pieces from the ragman, for Grandma was an expert on quilts and rugs. "My dear," she would say as we turned before her for admiration of a new dress, "how very pretty!" We always had the uncomfortable feeling that she did not see us inside the dress at all, but that her busy mind had already placed the material in quilt blocks or colorful patches in a hand-made rug.

It fell to the lot of the blue serge to become a rug. Many a time as I rested in bed with a cold or headache I would trace the blue lines around the bedside rug and relive the days of glory when that strip was with me in the flesh.

This spring Mother decided to replace the rugs with some of a less ancient vintage. I wondered if that would mean the passing of the blue serge.

"We need a new mattress for the porch bed," Mother declared one day. "Daddy, you might as well take some old clothes and these rag rugs up to the mattress factory." Now the eternal life of the serge is assured. When mattresses grow lumpy they can be put through the grinder again, and thus last for ever.

Mother was, I am sure, one of the pioneers in the field of the Indestructibility of Matter. She couldn't be bothered with such terms as indestructible. She merely said "durable." And she worked with blue serge instead of with equations.

Vol. 20, no. 7 (July 1933), pp. 437-38.

Vol. 18, no. 5 (May 1931), p. 298.

Many a Milestone Is Marked
With a Cross

By Caroline Eyring Miner

There were eight of us girls at the resort who "chummed to-gether." We laughed and danced and sang in the artificial hilarious way that was expected of us, and no one would have guessed that each girl guarded within her heart underneath her butterfly wings one of the world's troubles.

It is unusual the way in which these little trouble bugs that Pandora set free in the world have rested their wings and made their homes. They have not concentrated in any particular spot but have nested at random throughout the world.

On one particular evening after our work and entertaining was over, we eight girl chums, as usual, gathered together in one of the dormitory rooms for a little light chatter. And many times after the cocktail of light talk was over, the main course was served and we chatted in a more serious vein. This night in question our main talk turned at last to what we called our "secret sorrows," and strange to say there was not a single one of the eight girls who did not bare her heart and produce a family skeleton. One girl had a brother who was born an invalid, one girl had been told by a physician that she could never be a mother, one had a sister who had been born deaf, one an aged father who was blind, one had no parents, one a family hereditary tendency to insanity, and another a brother who was in the Federal prison.

97

After the talk was over and we had all wept, we felt united in
the common burden of the cross. Nature, or God, or whatever
we wish to name the distributor of crosses on humanity is no re-
specter of persons, and we who feel over-burdened and are har-
boring within our bosoms the venomous serpent, self-pity, need
only to look about us to see our neighbors one and all laboring
and straining under the load of even heavier burdens. And not a
few "but many a milestone is marked with a cross."

Vo. 21, no. 4 (Apr. 1934), p. 200.

Appreciation
By Valerie Peck

A few years ago a great scientist of nature, Luther Burbank,
conceived the idea of improving the standards of farm products.
His unique scheme in one case was to take what was best in several varieties of potatoes and unite them into one fine blend. People came to call this process of taking an ordinary variety and
grafting in desirable traits of other varieties "Burbanking."

It has dawned upon me, that, in a measure, is what Mother
has been trying to do to me. Using me, as I am, as the ordinary
scrub variety, she has drawn from the Relief Society ideas that
make for noble womanhood and has quietly gone about grafting
them into my make-up, "Burbanking" me. The process has not
been entirely painless, nor without opposition, and sometimes I
have been "Burbanked" in spite of furious resistance. But the
process continually goes on until I am beginning to find my outlook upon life taking a new meaning, a new richness, a new lus-
tre, through the "Burbanking" of Relief Society embellishments.
No one can come in contact with these, even second-hand, and
not be influenced by them. So through the Relief Society . . .
"Burbankings" I find that the undesirable scrub in me gradually
yields more easily each time to the finer, nobler, and more really
satisfying things of life.

Vol. 25, no. 1 (Jan. 1938), pp. 46-47.

The Song of the Lark

By Ivy Williams Stone

It was not there! I looked carefully around gallery 32 of the Chicago Art Institute. . . .

"I do not find Breton's 'Song of the Lark,' " I said. "Has it been moved to some other gallery?"

The guard did not slacken his measured steps, nor unfold his arms, nor even look at me.

"It's out on loan tour," he answered over his shoulder, as he walked toward another room.

"Oh!" I cried out.

But there was no one to share my disappointment. . . .

"Oh!" I repeated. "Why, I brought two children fifteen hundred miles to see that picture!"

I stood baffled, staring at the spot where the picture should have been. What should I tell the children? Their interest was spurred and fed by my enthusiasm. Only too well I knew they would find other diversions. My daughter wanted to attend a shoe sale at Marshall Field; my son hoped to see a sparring match between a jewfish and a shark in the Shedd Aquarium.

A gentle voice at my elbow brought me back to reality.

"Pardon me, Madam. . . . I heard what you said to the guard. The picture is not loaned. It is in retirement. You see, the Institute owns so many thousands of famous canvases, we have to rotate them. But fifteen hundred miles is a long distance, and your children must not be disappointed. I shall personally conduct them to the storage gallery. Shall we say, tomorrow, at ten?"

I looked into the smiling face of a man so delicately molded, it seemed he had stepped down from one of the decorative pieces of priceless china. . . .

Back in the hotel, I schooled the children all evening, so they would be appreciative of this unusual service.

"The shoe sale will be over by the time we get there," protested my daughter. "I did so want a pair of those open-toed, patent leather, French heels. There isn't a store in our state that carries the style I want. What's an old picture, anyway?"

Promptly at ten the next morning we reported to the little man at his desk in gallery 32. . . .

We went along hallways, where uniformed guards touched their caps, as they unlocked gates for us. Finally we came to the aisle marked "French: 19th century."

At a signal from our guide, a guard unlocked the final gate, and we were ushered into an air-cooled, tomblike room, lined with rows upon rows of portable racks.

"Breton," spoke our guide, and a button was pushed. A rack rolled out. Another button, and the large canvas of "The Song of the Lark" stood out alone. It was illuminated. I was suddenly happy, for both children were awed.

There stood the peasant girl, with her coarse garments, her huge, hardened bare feet, the strength of her sickle hand plainly revealed. The lark was soaring from its nesting place in the brown furrow; with a song on her own lips, the girl watched its ascent. Health was evident in every line of her body, as though born of the green meadow and the brown earth of the field. The sun, just rising over the distant treetops, illumined her face. From her snooded hair to her feet she revealed contentment and peace. The green meadow, the freshly plowed furrows, the azure sky, all climaxed her inexplicable smile.

The children studied the picture and listened to a half-hour discourse on the works of Breton, artist and poet. As they studied the picture, I studied its effect upon them. My faith was vindicated. The delicate voice of our guide recited some of Breton's poetry. Born a French peasant, Breton had lived in the deep poverty of the down-trodden poor. . . . He excelled in depicting the despair of the country folk. A painter of rustic life, a man of the poor. . . .

As we retraced our course, gates were locked behind us. Up elevators, along steel-barred halls, and finally out into the light of the galleries, we went. My son's demonstration of courtesy, his speech of thanks to our kindly guide, gave me added joy in being his mother.

My adolescent daughter had a dreamy, faraway expression in her eyes. She looked at her trimly shod feet and whispered to me: "All she ever had were wooden clogs."

Our guide gave me his card, shook hands all around, and quickly left us.

We sauntered through gallery after gallery. The children, rather than I, wanted to see more. The guard was doing his paces from room to room. His arms were folded, his face bored.

As we stood on the front steps of the Institute, flanked by the guarding lions, I glanced at my watch.

"We still have time to get to Marshall Field," I said to my daughter. "Perhaps you can yet find what you want in shoes. And I feel sure the Shedd Aquarium will be open this afternoon."

She glanced at her sensible, durable, walking oxfords. "These are good enough," she smiled. "I guess French heels would be hard to walk in."

"What's a couple of sparring fish?" countered my son. "Heigh," he queried, "who was that little man, anyway? What's his name?"

I held the card in my palm, and all three of us looked at the printing. Our guide had been an assistant curator of the Chicago Art Institute.

Vol. 36, no. 3 (Mar. 1949), pp. 156-59.

Vol. 23, no. 3 (Mar. 1936), p. 271.

Gardening—Food for the Soul

By Pauline M. Henderson

"Your yard always looks so nice," my next-door neighbor greeted me the other morning. "But it must be such a lot of work for you."

Her words struck me with a little shock of surprise, for I have never considered my gardening in terms of "work." . . .

Can it be considered work, I wondered, to come out of the house in the glow of early morning, and with a hoe gently disturb the cool, chocolate-colored earth around rosebushes fragrant with blossoms? And where is the drudgery in pushing a spade deep into the yielding soil, while the friendly sun warms one's back and shoulders—almost like a benediction from the heavens?

My garden is much, much more to me than a mere section of planted space around my home. It is, indeed, many things.

It can be a release from pent-up tension and frustration. . . . As I strike my hoe into the earth, each weed is an enemy going down to destruction. By the time the bed is clear of weeds, the tension is gone, and I am able to face the problem—whatever it may be—with new calmness.

102

Of all the activities involved in the making of a home, the planting of the garden is by far the most rewarding. I can spend hours cleaning the house, only to realize that in a few days I shall have to do it all over again. But the time I spend in the garden will show results for an entire season, perhaps even for years.

A garden can be just as surely a medium for self-expression as the painting of a picture or the writing of a poem. And no special talent is needed. A garden asks only loving care, and it will flourish and bloom for you, whether you be rich or poor, obscure or famous.

There is a lesson in faith to be learned from plants. Someone once said, "To tend a garden is to walk with God." Certainly a wavering faith cannot help but be strengthened as one watches a seed grow from a tiny, inanimate object to a living, flourishing plant. . . .

A garden teaches patience. Growing things will not be hurried. . . . I have often reflected, as I set out young plants, and felt the rich dark earth between my fingers, for how many ages has this self-same earth existed—how many more it will still exist! And I find my own petty troubles fading into relative insignificance. . . .

Once, when a particularly dark cloud was shadowing my life, and there seemed no hope that I would ever again come through into the sunshine, I happened to glance from my window at the flowering peach tree I had planted some years before. It was in the full glory of spring bloom . . . breathtakingly beautiful. Suddenly, I found myself remembering how that same tree looked in mid-winter—bare, gray branches . . . stark and dreary, giving not the slightest hint of the beauty that in just a few short months would burst forth. And I felt a sudden rebirth of hope surge within me. I thought, just as that tree has come from ugliness to beauty, so will this darkness eventually give way to light. And I found new courage to go on.

My garden is not the most beautiful in the neighborhood. To me it is not necessary that it should be. My grass is not the greenest nor my flowers the largest or most colorful. But I am content. . . .

No, I cannot agree with my neighbor that gardening is work. Rather it is living in its truest sense.

Vol. 39, no. 3 (Mar. 1952), pp. 196-97.

Way Down Inside

By Margaret Lundstrom

"There's a homely little fellow!" The woman in front of me nudged her companion as she spoke.

"I should say so!" came the reply. "Like a mud fence, he is."

Jimmy walked on across the stage, his straight little body intent as he carried the Cub Scout banner proudly.

Is Jimmy homely? I wondered. I'd never thought so. And if Tom had, he'd never told me. Wouldn't we know, when we'd looked at him every day for eight years?

Think of the way he got up in the morning, his eyes bright from sleep as he chirped, "Good morning, Mother, I love you!" or the smile he gave the doctor when he was told he had the mumps, and it was the day before the school picnic.

"It hurts so much to smile," he said, his voice a whisper, since it had to squeeze past the lump in his throat, "that I guess I couldn't probably stand it to cry, so that's why I'm not."

And the day Annie left the gate open, and the puppy got out, and the busy street with its inevitable car. I dreaded telling him, piling his heartache and tears on top of my own. But he put his arm about my shoulders and rubbed his snubby, freckled nose against my cheek and whispered, "That's all right, Mommy. Don't cry."

I looked again at Jimmy as he stood there on the stage, over at one side, now. And then I looked at the backs of the women in front of me, and I thought: you don't really see Jimmy. If you did . . .

And all the way home, walking along the shaded streets with his plump sticky little fingers entwined through mine, I kept trying to think of something. Something like "Beauty is only skin deep," only, of course, that wasn't it. The irony of it made me chuckle. Jimmy's fingers squeezed mine and his round face turned up to me.

"You're laughing at yourself, aren't you, Mom?"

"Yes. But how'd you know?"

He skipped twice on one foot, and sculled a stray leaf from the toe of one shoe.

"W-e-e-l-l . . ." he drawled thoughtfully, "it came from way down inside you." He skipped again. "And it was quiet, like nobody else had to hear if they didn't want to."

It was after that, maybe a dozen steps nearer home, that I felt the pity. It was a heavy thing in my chest, and it was for those two women who had sat in front of me who hadn't been able to see a little boy's beautiful heart because it lay behind a plain, little face.

Vol. 41, no. 3 (Mar. 1954), p. 205.

On Second Thought

By Stella Hatch

In this tension-filled whirl we live in, I've found an oasis. It is second thought. I cannot tell exactly when I discovered it, but it has saved me untold anxiety. I can truthfully say it has given me peace of mind.

Take, for example, money. I used to spend it when I had it and hardly knew where it went, or whether it would reach or not. Now I plan for it. Then, on second thought, I replan it and it reaches, because I find things there that I can very well do without. It is a big relief when I do. When my children must have this or that luxury, I very firmly give it my second thought and let the children work for the money. They appreciate it more.

Just last week I planned an evening at the movie for me and the children; then, on second thought, I bought ice cream cones for us and our new neighbor's children, and we spent two wonderful hours getting acquainted.

I have been accomplishing my work by doing certain things

on certain days and have been nervous and upset when anything interfered. On second thought, I sat down and made a list of the things I just *had* to do to keep a moderately clean house, a well-fed family, and presentable washings and ironings. Then I listed all the extras I have been tearing my heart out about and put each one down on a separate recipe card. Now, I take one of them out every day and work on it for ninety minutes; then I have the rest of the day to live and love more than I have ever done. I am accomplishing more, I'm not worrying about what hasn't been done, because I know that someday soon the card will pop up, and I enjoy my family so much more. Of course, they are wondering what has happened to me, but I just smile and squeeze my file box.

When traveling I choose a route. On second thought, I consider what I shall miss by going that way, so I reroute to have more pleasure for the same amount of gas.

I have been upset many times in disciplining the children, even punishing the wrong one. Now, on second thought, I am beginning to use more reason and much prayer. My children are slowly responding to my change of attitude. I have found myself becoming more patient.

My husband and I have been happier together, because when I have become annoyed about something, I give it a second thought, of what tomorrow would be like if he were taken from me. I try to greet him with a smile and appreciate the wonderful man he is. The petty things just seem to fade out. Try second thought. It is soul-satisfying.

Vol. 48, no. 4 (Apr. 1961), p. 278.

My Testimony

By Alice Louise Reynolds

My parting word is this: I have heard so much talk about thrills—we have worn that word threadbare—thrills in art. We want to know if the newest play and the newest book has a thrill. What are all the thrills of earth? What, indeed, are the thrills of science, for the scientists tell us there is no thrill equal to discovering a new truth, but I will tell you the thrill that I think is above and beyond all other thrills. I heard President Joseph F. Smith say at one time, when the light from the window poured across the audience, "There isn't a person in the audience but what can see that stream of light. I know that God lives better than I know that light enters this building. I know it better than I know any other thing in all this world." And the power with which he bore that testimony caused a thrill to run through his audience. I have heard hundreds of people testify to it.

These are the thrills that are worthwhile, the thrills that have no bitter dregs. So, my sisters, do not envy the great of the world; do not think that it would be above and beyond all else to be an Edison. We all thank God for Edison, but in this world that is starved for spirituality, where the famine for the word of God is greater than it is for wheat in the famine-stricken districts, any human being who stands up with courage testifying of God, testifying that the gospel has been restored, makes a contribution to the world that no one can value, and my prayer is that the Spirit of the Lord may be with us, that that contribution which it is ours to give may become greater and mightier as the days roll on.

Vol. 9, no. 12 (Dec. 1922), p. 636.

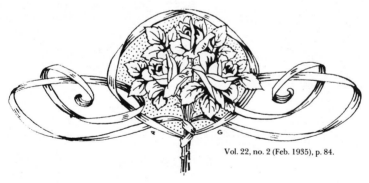

Vol. 22, no. 2 (Feb. 1935), p. 84.

From Near and Far

A new feature—"From Near and Far"—makes its first appearance with this issue of the magazine. This page is designed to feature comments from readers, notes about authors, and other items of interest. Readers are invited to submit brief paragraphs of opinions, suggestions, and interesting notes "From Near and Far."

Vol. 35, no. 4 (Apr. 1948), p. 249.

My husband who was recalled into the Marine Corps is being sent to Korea, so I will be moving into Los Angeles to await his return. I would like to tell you how much I love the magazine and what it has meant to me. Realizing the mixed emotions that would be in my heart during this crucial time, before I left Salt Lake City, I gathered up my grandmother's and my *Relief Society Magazines* for the past four years and brought them with me. With their help, I have been studying Dr. Talmage's *Jesus the Christ*. What a blessing this has been to me. It has strengthened my testimony, given me a deeper insight into the divinity of the works of Jesus, and been a source of information and strength in helping my husband at this time.

FLORENCE C. JOHNSON
San Clemente, California

Vol. 38, no. 8 (Aug. 1951), p. 576.

I like the *Relief Society Magazine* very much. I have been confined to my bed for the past ten years with arthritis, so am unable to take an active part in the Church, and so am most happy to have the magazine.

RHODA BRYANT
Basalt, Idaho

Vol. 39, no. 1 (Jan. 1952), p. 72.

Thanks so much for the wonderful magazine. It helped me through many a lonely time when I was single. It contains beautiful stories that can uplift the soul of a lonely soldier far from home. Thanks again for the wonderful sisters of Relief Society.

SGT. BRENT BOEHME
Denver, Colorado

Vol. 56, no. 12 (Dec. 1969), p. 882.

My mother read the magazine to me when I lived at home, and I experimented with some of the recipes. While I was in the mission field the magazine was a regular part of my proselyting tools—it was, so to speak, my second "companion." Now I am a young housewife and a regular subscriber to the magazine for myself—and how very precious it is in my home. I read every printed word, absorbing every ounce of love that is contained within the covers. The only problem now is that I have a stiff competitor for the magazine's attentions—my husband. When I was married I was proud of the lovely dowry of handwork I brought to our new home. My husband, on the other hand, had been a regular subscriber to the magazine throughout college, the service, and his mission, and brought to our home bound copies of each issue since 1954!

NADINE H. KERR
San Jose, California

Vol. 57, no. 2 (Feb. 1970), p. 82.

The magazine comes to me as a gift from a dear friend. . . . Every issue is just wonderful from cover to cover. The articles, stories, and poems are inspiring; the art layouts and illustrations are delightful. Many of the recipes have become family favorites.

Most precious to me, though, are the lessons. I am not a member of your church, but four of our seven children are active and enthusiastic Latter-day Saints. It is my constant and fervent prayer that some day it will be possible for the rest of my family, including myself, to be baptized into the Church.

BETH RAEHL
Larsen, Wisconsin

Vol. 57, no. 4 (Apr. 1970), p. 242.

I really enjoyed the article on sourdough ("Make a New Start with Alaskan Sourdough" by Edythe K. Watson, February 1970). While on Okinawa we were given a start of 1898 Alaska strain by our district president C. Wayne Jenkins. In June, just before we left Okinawa, the start was accidentally thrown out. We missed our sourdough. Later, after returning home, I was in a doctor's office and the subject of sourdough came up. The doctor, a woman, then recounted how a Mormon friend and former missionary to Alaska had given her a start of this 1898 strain when they were neighbors in Nashville, Tennessee. To make a long story short, 10,000 miles from the place of our first start, we were given a replacement of the same strain. It's a small world—I wonder where else this former missionary's sourdough has been.

JUDITH L. GASKIN
Rockville, Maryland

Vol. 57, no. 5 (May 1970), p. 322.

To me, the *Relief Society Magazine* is like clear water in a dark desert. There are already enough magazines that "tell it like it is." I am grateful for a magazine that "tells it like it should be." I testify that the spirit of Relief Society rides with its magazine to all corners of the world and blesses all it reaches.

SHERRY DOWNING
Sewell, New Jersey

Vol. 57, no. 7 (July 1970), p. 482.

ATTENTION SISTERS!

Subscribe NOW for the MAGAZINE

N account of the shortage of paper and the heavy increase of all press work, it will be impossible to publish only such numbers of the *Magazine* as are actually subscribed for.   Therefore, our friends must send in their subscriptions at once.

Who among you can get along without the *RELIEF SOCIETY MAGAZINE?*

It will be impossible to supply back numbers. If you want the January number you must send in your names before December 15.

GET BUSY, AGENTS!

SUBSCRIBE FOR THE

Relief Society

MAGAZINE

~~~~~~~~~~

EIGHT REASONS

Why You Should Have This Magazine in Your Home:

1. It is the OFFICIAL ORGAN OF THE RELIEF SO-CIETY.

2. Its pages will be graced with the writings of our be-loved President, Emmeline B. Wells.

3. It will have CURRENT EVENTS treated by a bril-liant editorial writer.

4. In NOTES FROM THE FIELD will appear items of general and particular interest from every stake and mission of the Church.

5. The Guide lessons will be given in each Magazine.

6. Stories and poems will vary the more serious accounts of our work.

7. There will be departments on Genealogy, Clothing for Women, Health, Cookery, Books, Art in the Home, and Amuse-ments.

8. The price is ONLY one dollar a year.

Subscribe NOW.

Subscriptions to be paid in advance.

Index

THE
RELIEF
SOCIETY
MAGAZINE

VOL. XXIII   MARCH 1936   NO. 3

The
RELIEF SOCIETY
Magazine

Volume XXIII   AUGUST, 1928   No. 8

The
RELIEF SOCIETY
Magazine

September 1928   Vol. XV No. 9

The
RELIEF SOCIETY
Magazine

Volume XXI   MARCH, 1934   No. 3

BIRTHPLACE OF THE RELIEF SOCIETY
MT. PLEASANT, UTAH

The RELIEF SOCIETY
MAGAZINE

CONFERENCE ISSUE

VOL. 28 NO. 12   December 3rd March   DECEMBER 1940

The
RELIEF SOCIETY
Magazine

Volume XXI   SEPTEMBER, 1934   No. 9

CONFERENCE NUMBER

The RELIEF SOCIETY
MAGAZINE

MARCH 1940   VOL. XXVII NO. 3

LOOKING FORWARD

The
RELIEF SOCIETY
Magazine

Volume XXI   OCTOBER, 1934   No. 10

The RELIEF SOCIETY
MAGAZINE

CONFERENCE
ISSUE

NOVEMBER 1940   VOL. XXVII NO. 11

The
RELIEF SOCIETY
Magazine

Volume XXI   DECEMBER, 1934   No. 12

The RELIEF SOCIETY
MAGAZINE

BENEVOLENCE

NOVEMBER 1940

THROUGH LOVE SERVE ONE ANOTHER

The
RELIEF SOCIETY
Magazine

Volume XXIII   NOVEMBER, 1928   No. 11